HUNGARY 2016 HUMAN RIGHTS REPORT

EXECUTIVE SUMMARY

Hungary is a multiparty parliamentary democracy. The unicameral National Assembly (parliament) exercises legislative authority. The parliament elects the president (the head of state) every five years. The president appoints a prime minister from the majority party or coalition in parliament following national elections every four years. In the 2014 parliamentary elections, the center-right Fidesz-KDNP (Christian Democratic People's Party) alliance retained a two-thirds majority in parliament, receiving 45 percent of party-list votes while winning 91 percent of the country's single-member districts allocated through a first-past-the-post system. The governing coalition lost its two-thirds majority in parliament in March 2015. The Organization for Security and Cooperation in Europe (OSCE) election observation mission's report concluded the elections were efficiently administered and offered voters a diverse choice following an inclusive candidate registration process, although the main governing party enjoyed an undue advantage because of restrictive campaign regulations, biased media coverage, and campaign activities that blurred the separation between political party and the state. Viktor Orban, the Fidesz party leader, has been prime minister since 2010.

Civilian authorities maintained effective control over security forces.

The most significant human rights problem remained the government's handling of migrants and asylum seekers seeking to transit the country, which was marked by several reports of physical abuse and xenophobic rhetoric. International organizations and human rights nongovernmental organizations (NGOs) continued to voice criticism of the systematic erosion of the rule of law; potential violations of international humanitarian law; weakening of checks and balances, democratic institutions, and transparency; and intimidation of independent societal voices since 2010.

Other human rights problems included prison overcrowding and substandard physical conditions, physical abuse of prisoners and detainees by prison and detention staff, prisoner-on-prisoner violence, a politically determined process for government registration of religious groups, government corruption, growing media concentration that restricted editorial independence, and governmental pressure on civil society. There were reports of domestic violence against women and children, sexual harassment of women, anti-Semitism, abuse and inhuman treatment of institutionalized children and persons with mental and physical disabilities, social exclusion and discrimination against Roma, and trafficking in persons.

There were allegations of physical abuse of migrants and asylum seekers entering irregularly by security forces, particularly during push-backs across the border, but the government resisted calls to order an independent investigation into the reports. Civil society organizations widely suspected impunity among government officials and public employees involved in corruption.

Section 1. Respect for the Integrity of the Person, Including Freedom from:

a. Arbitrary Deprivation of Life and other Unlawful or Politically Motivated Killings

On November 12, the Central Investigative Prosecutor's Office launched an investigation for mistreatment in an official proceeding against four prison officers in connection with the death of a 44-year-old prisoner on the same day in the Budapest High and Medium Security Prison. On November 17, the prison commander suspended the four prison wardens and one other staff member at the medical unit for two months and launched disciplinary procedures against them (see also section 1.c., Prison and Detention Center Conditions).

On March 31, Bela Biszku, who had been under prosecution since 2013 for acting as an accomplice to war crimes and multiple murders committed by the government during the communist era, died at the age of 94, which terminated the pending court case.

b. Disappearance

There were no reports of politically motivated disappearances.

c. Torture and Other Cruel, Inhuman, or Degrading Treatment or Punishment

The constitution and law prohibit such practices, but there were reports that authorities did not always observe these prohibitions.

As of September, the commissioner for fundamental rights (ombudsman) issued seven reports within the framework of the national preventive mechanism of the Optional Protocol to the UN Convention against Torture (OPCAT) on unannounced site inspections in detention facilities. The inspected institutions included penitentiaries, police holding facilities, homes for the elderly, and centers for children with disabilities or special needs. All these reports established cases of cruel, inhuman, or degrading treatment or punishment.

Since June the Office of the UN High Commissioner for Refugees (UNHCR), the Hungarian Helsinki Committee (HHC), Human Rights Watch (HRW), and Amnesty International released reports on allegations of abuse and violence by law enforcement officials against migrants and asylum seekers who entered the country irregularly from Serbia. The reports included allegations of systemic violence, including bites by unleashed dogs, the use of pepper spray, beatings with truncheons, and other mistreatment. On July 15, UNHCR called on the government to investigate reports of abuses. As of November, there was no official information on any internal investigations having been opened based on the abuse allegations.

On June 4, UNHCR reported the case of a 22-year-old Syrian man who drowned in the Tisza River on June 1 after uniformed personnel allegedly pushed him back to prevent his crossing the border illegally from Serbia. The HHC reported that police opened a public administration proceeding on the basis of unnatural death and, separately, the Szeged Investigative Prosecutor's Office began a criminal investigation against unknown perpetrators for mistreatment during official proceedings. Police terminated the public administration proceeding on September 26. On October 25, the prosecutor's office terminated the investigation based on lack of evidence that a crime had been committed. On December 21, the HHC filed a complaint against the prosecutorial decision to terminate the investigation, which remained pending at the Office of the Prosecutor General.

Prison and Detention Center Conditions

Overcrowding and poor physical conditions remained problematic in the prison system, potentially subjecting inmates to inhuman and degrading treatment. There were occasional reports of physical violence by prison guards; prisoner-on-prisoner violence; and instances of authorities holding pretrial detainees and convicted prisoners together, as well as juveniles with adults.

<u>Physical Conditions</u>: The HHC reported that the high level of overcrowding in penitentiaries continued to constitute a serious human rights problem.

As of November 8, there were 18,146 inmates in prisons and detention centers, including 1,333 women and 299 juveniles; the official capacity of these facilities was 13,771. The prison population increased to 132 percent of capacity, compared with 127 percent at the end of 2015. On March 7, the Council of Europe released its annual penal statistics report, which stated that the country's prisons were severely overcrowded, with an occupancy rate of 142 percent in 2014.

On January 7, the European Court of Human Rights (ECHR) ruled in five cases of 49 prisoners, ordering the government to pay 692,000 euros ($761,000) in compensation for degrading treatment due to overcrowding and unsanitary conditions. In March 2015 the ECHR issued a pilot judgment in a similar case of six prisoners and concluded that the overcrowding of penitentiaries was a structural problem in the country. The ECHR consequently called on the government to produce a timeframe for introducing preventive and compensatory remedies that would provide effective redress for human rights violations stemming from prison overcrowding. On October 25, parliament amended the law, effective January 2017, to introduce state compensation of 1,200 to 1,600 forints ($4.30-5.70) per day to prisoners for degrading treatment due to overcrowding and unsanitary conditions. Detainees must request such compensation at the prison of their detention within six months of the termination of the holding conditions that violated fundamental rights, and a judge specializing in detention decides the claim. In response to the newly introduced domestic remedies, on November 8, the ECHR decided to suspend until August 2017 the pending applications brought before the court, numbering approximately 6,800, concerning conditions of detention.

On May 23, the ombudsman released an OPCAT report on the Somogy County Prison in Kaposvar that strongly criticized the practice of ordering prisoners in groups to undress in the prison's chapel for full body searches. The report also noted poor physical and hygienic conditions; prisoner-on-prisoner violence; verbal and physical violence against inmates by one prison warden; racism and sexism by several prison wardens; and the failure to separate minor and adult inmates.

A 2010 order of the national police chief requires law enforcement personnel to be present when medical staff examine detainees, making exceptions only when the inmate or doctor so requests and if permitted by the senior guard supervisor. The HHC continued to object that detainees who alleged physical mistreatment usually were examined only by internal medical staff. According to the HHC, security personnel were present less frequently during medical examinations in penitentiary institutions.

As of November 25, 53 deaths took place in prisons and six in pretrial detention. Of the 59 deaths, 51 were natural deaths and seven were suicides. In each case, internal investigations followed the incident but, as of November 28, no staff member of the penitentiary has been found responsible.

On November 12, the Central Investigative Prosecutor's Office launched an investigation for mistreatment in an official proceeding against four prison officers in connection with the death of a 44-year-old prisoner on November 12 in the Budapest High and Medium Security Prison. On November 17, the prison commander suspended the four prison wardens and one other staff member at the medical unit for two months and launched disciplinary procedures against them (see also section 1.a.).

The HHC continued to report unsatisfactory physical conditions in certain penitentiaries, including the presence of bedbugs and other insects. Sanitation and toilet facilities were also poor and insufficient in number in some cases. In some prisons, toilets were not separated from living spaces. The HHC also noted frequent shortages in natural light and artificial lighting in cells and a lack of adequate heating. There continued to be a shortage of psychological care.

Administration: NGOs reported that authorities occasionally failed to investigate fully credible allegations of mistreatment. There was no separate ombudsperson for prisons, but detainees could submit complaints to the commissioner for fundamental rights (ombudsman) or to the prosecutor's office responsible for supervising the lawfulness of detention. The ombudsman handled prison complaints and conducted ex officio inquiries but had no authority to act on behalf of prisoners.

Independent Monitoring: The National Police Headquarters (ORFK) permitted independent monitoring of detention conditions by the HHC and international human rights groups. The HHC carried out regular monitoring visits to penal institutions based on a cooperation agreement concluded with the National Penitentiary Headquarters. The HHC reported that it conducted four visits to prisons through the end of October.

Improvements: During the year prison capacity increased by 146 inmate spaces, reducing overcrowding.

d. Arbitrary Arrest or Detention

The constitution and law prohibit arbitrary arrest and detention. There were reports authorities did not always observe these prohibitions.

Role of the Police and Security Apparatus

The ORFK, under the direction of the minister of interior, is responsible for maintaining order nationwide. The country's 19 county police departments and the Budapest police headquarters are directly subordinate to the ORFK. City police have local jurisdiction but are subordinate to the county police. Two other units are directly subordinate to the minister of interior: the Counterterrorism Center (commonly known by its Hungarian acronym "TEK") and the National Protective Service (NPS). The TEK is responsible for protecting the prime minister and the president and for preventing, uncovering, and detecting terrorist acts, including kidnappings, hijackings, and other offenses related to such acts, and arresting the perpetrators. The NPS is responsible for preventing and detecting internal corruption in law enforcement agencies, government administrative agencies, and civilian secret services. Both the TEK and the NPS are empowered to gather intelligence and conduct undercover policing, in certain cases without prior judicial authorization.

Concerning the national intelligence services, the Constitution Protection Office and the Special Service for National Security are under the supervision of the minister of interior and responsible for domestic intelligence.

On June 7, parliament adopted a law creating a new national security service entity, the Counterterrorism Information and Crime Analysis Center (TIBEK), under the direct supervision of the minister of interior. TIBEK can establish unlimited connections between its data management system and that of the other intelligence agencies. TIBEK has no authority to conduct secret information gathering activities and has no access to information collected by the NPS on police officers. TIBEK started operation on July 7.

The Hungarian Defense Force is subordinate to the Ministry of Defense and is responsible for external security as well as aspects of domestic security and disaster response. Since September 2015, under a declared state of emergency prompted by mass migration, defense forces may assist law enforcement forces in border protection and handling mass migration (see also section 2.d., Access to Asylum).

On June 7, parliament amended the constitution to create a new "threat of terror" state of emergency. Under the provision, in the event of an act of terror or its considerable and immediate danger, parliament, at the initiative of the cabinet, can declare a state of emergency due to a threat of terror with the support of two-thirds of members of parliament present. After the cabinet initiates the announcement of the special legal order at parliament, the cabinet can issue decrees to suspend the application of or to derogate from certain laws, or take other extraordinary measures for up to 15 days before the special legal order must be confirmed by a two-thirds parliamentary vote. Such measures may include tightening border controls, transferring air traffic control to the military, deploying armed forces and law enforcement forces to protect critical infrastructure, and taking special counterterrorism measures. The amendment specifies that the cabinet can deploy armed forces domestically only if the use of law enforcement and national intelligence agencies are insufficient under the threat of terror.

Organized citizen groups, such as neighborhood and town watches, played a significant role in helping police prevent crime and maintain public security. The law requires neighborhood watch groups to complete a formal cooperation agreement with relevant police departments and imposes fines for any failure of cooperation. The prosecutor's office maintained legal control over the operation of the neighborhood watch groups and could initiate legal proceedings in court if a group lacked a formal cooperation agreement with police.

Civilian authorities generally maintained effective control over law enforcement and the armed forces, and the government had effective mechanisms to investigate and punish abuse and corruption. Military prosecutors are responsible for investigating abuses by military, police, penitentiary staff, parliamentary guards, clandestine services, and disaster units.

There were reports of impunity involving security forces during the year, concerning allegations of abuse and violence by law enforcement officials against migrants and asylum seekers entering the country irregularly from Serbia (see section 1.c.). The HHC also noted a large disparity between the number of indictments of official persons (such as police officers and penitentiary staff) alleged to have committed abuses and the indictment of persons alleged to have committed violent acts against officials. Through the end of October, approximately 4.8 percent of complaints of mistreatment in official proceedings by members of the security forces resulted in indictments, while 69 percent of alleged acts of violence against official persons resulted in indictments.

The HHC also criticized the right of the minister of interior to determine the eligibility of police officers and penitentiary staff members to continue service in their full capacities after being convicted of crimes, including mistreatment of defendants during official proceedings or forced interrogation. In 2015 the minister permitted four police officers convicted for mistreatment in official proceedings and two officers convicted for forced interrogation to continue in service.

Arrest Procedures and Treatment of Detainees

Police are obligated to take into "short-term arrest" individuals who are apprehended committing a crime or are subject to an arrest warrant. Police may take into short-term arrest individuals who are suspected of having committed a crime or a petty offense or are unable or unwilling to identify themselves. Police may also take into short-term arrest unaccompanied minors who are suspected of having run away from parental authority or guardianship. Short-term arrests generally last up to eight hours but may last up to 12 hours in exceptional cases. Police may hold persons under "detention for the purposes of public safety" for 24 hours if the identification of the person concerned so requires. Detention of conditionally released persons who abscond from probation, or may reasonably be expected to do so, may last up to 72 hours. Police, a prosecutor, or a judge may order detention of suspects for 72 hours if there is a well-founded suspicion of an offense that is punishable by imprisonment and the subsequent pretrial detention of the defendant appears likely. A prosecutor must file a motion with an investigatory judge requesting pretrial detention prior to the lapse of the 72-hour detention or release the detainee. A defendant may appeal a pretrial detention order.

Police must inform suspects of the charges against them at the beginning of their first interrogation, which must be within 24 hours of detention. Authorities generally respected this right.

There is a functioning bail system. According to the HHC, bail and other alternatives to pretrial detention were underused.

By law, police must inform suspects of their right to counsel before questioning them. Representation by defense counsel is mandatory in the investigative phase if suspects face a charge punishable by more than five years' imprisonment; are already incarcerated; are deaf, blind, unable to speak, or have a mental disability; are unfamiliar with the Hungarian language or the language of the procedure; are unable to defend themselves in person for any reason; are juveniles; or are indigent and request the appointment of a defense counsel. When defense counsel is required, suspects have three days to hire an attorney, otherwise police or the prosecutor appoint one. If suspects make clear their unwillingness to retain counsel, police or the prosecutor are required to appoint counsel (ex officio) immediately by choosing a lawyer from a list kept by a competent bar association. The HHC continued to criticize the system of ex officio legal representation on the basis that the quality of "in-house" ex officio defense counsels appointed by authorities was generally substandard.

By law, neither police nor the prosecutor are obligated to wait for counsel to arrive before interrogating a suspect. In 2013 the Constitutional Court noted that the absence of mandatory defense counsel at the first interrogation of a criminal suspect due to police failure to provide timely notification of the date and place of the session violated the constitutional right to defense counsel. The court ruled that any statement made by a suspect in the absence of legal counsel may not be considered as evidence during the criminal proceeding. Human rights NGOs continued to report, however, that police routinely proceeded with interrogation in the absence of defense counsel immediately after notifying suspects of their right to counsel.

The law permits short-term detainees to notify relatives or others of their detention within eight hours unless the notification would jeopardize the investigation. Investigative authorities must notify relatives of a person under "72-hour detention" of the detention and the detainee's location within 24 hours. A 2014 report by the Council of Europe's Committee for the Prevention of Torture (CPT) noted a lack of immediate notification of relatives of those in 72-hour detention and criticized the 24-hour deadline as excessively long.

Arbitrary Arrest: There were reports of arbitrary arrests. During the first eight months of the year, the Office of the Prosecutor General initiated indictment in one case of alleged arbitrary arrest, rejected official complaints of arbitrary detention in 30 cases, and closed the investigations without filing charges in 15 cases.

Pretrial Detention: Under certain conditions (involving a risk of a detainee escaping, committing a new offense, reoffending, hindering an investigation, or colluding with co-perpetrators), a prosecutor may file a motion with an investigatory judge to order pretrial detention. Criminal proceedings for cases where the accused is in pretrial detention take priority over other types of expedited hearings. A detainee may appeal pretrial detention.

The HHC reported that authorities generally failed to conduct procedures in a timely manner and with due diligence for defendants in pretrial detention. The law, in certain cases, does not limit the duration of pretrial detention, including when the criminal offense is punishable by more than 15 years' imprisonment, pending a trial court judgment. In March 2015 the ombudsman initiated a case at the Constitutional Court that would restore the general four-year limit on pretrial detention that was in effect prior to 2013 for persons accused of crimes punishable by imprisonment for more than 15 years. The Constitutional Court's response remained pending at the end of November.

The HHC reported there was a 24 percent decrease in prosecutorial motions seeking a court order of pretrial detention from 2013 to 2015. The number of pretrial detainees was 21 percent lower at the end of 2015 compared to the end of 2013. According to the HHC, prosecutorial motions to order pretrial detention during the investigative phase of the proceeding had a success rate greater than 90 percent in many counties, with a national success rate of 87.7 percent in 2015. According to the National Penitentiary Headquarters, as of November 8, authorities held 3,228 persons in pretrial detention, which was 17.7 percent of the overall number of people in detention. Of these, 704 had been incarcerated for six months to a year and 603 had been held for more than a year.

Detainee's Ability to Challenge Lawfulness of Detention before a Court: The defendant, defense council, or prosecution in a judicial proceeding may at any point move to have the defendant released from pretrial detention. The court must examine the motion on its merits and make a reasoned decision. The defendant may submit a complaint to police or the prosecution against the decision when placed in 72-hour detention. Submitting such a complaint does not suspend detention. Any person who believes that short-term arrest by police violates his or her fundamental rights may file a complaint with the police unit responsible or with the independent police complaints board.

The law provides that persons held in pretrial detention or under house arrest and later acquitted may receive monetary compensation.

Protracted Detention of Rejected Asylum Seekers or Stateless Persons: The law permits the detention of rejected asylum seekers who were in detention during their asylum procedure and whose deportation was pending or who declined to leave the country voluntarily within a prescribed period. Authorities may also order the detention of rejected asylum seekers whom authorities suspect are at risk of fleeing following the rejection of their asylum application. Authorities may place rejected asylum seekers in "immigration detention" for a maximum of 12 months (30 days in cases of families with children).

The HHC reported that immigration detention generally took place in immigration detention centers. The HHC continued to criticize the general practice of placing handcuffs and leashes on immigrant detainees when they leave detention center premises under police escort or with armed security guards without any individualized assessment of the risk posed by the individual.

e. Denial of Fair Public Trial

The constitution and law provide for an independent judiciary. Courts often functioned independently, but attempts to exert political influence over the judiciary occurred. NGOs and international organizations continued to assert that laws on the judicial system adopted in 2011-13 contributed to weakened checks and balances by restricting the competence of the Constitutional Court, altering rules for electing Constitutional Court justices, and vesting the president of the National Office for the Judiciary (NOJ) with significant decision-making power. Government officials occasionally publicly criticized nonfinal court rulings.

By law, the Constitutional Court does not have competence to review potentially unconstitutional legislation with budgetary impact if the legislation is adopted when the state debt exceeds 50 percent of GDP. This limitation remains in effect for previously adopted laws, even if the state debt were to fall below 50 percent. The law provides that a committee consisting of members of party factions proportionate to their representation in parliament has the right to nominate, with a two-thirds majority, a Constitutional Court justice. A two-thirds majority in parliament must endorse a nominee in order to be elected as a Constitutional Court justice, whose term is 12 years. Prior to the governing coalition's loss of its two-thirds majority in parliament in March 2015, the law allowed the governing parties the necessary two-thirds majority in both the nominating committee and the assembly. During this period, the Fidesz-KDNP majority elected 12 Constitutional Court justices. As of April 21, four of the 15 seats were vacant (including that of the court president) following the end of the terms of sitting justices. On November 22, parliament elected four new justices and a new court president to the Constitutional Court upon the joint nomination of the governing parties and the opposition Politics Can Be Different party.

On June 23, the ECHR confirmed in a final ruling that the dismissal of Andras Baka in 2011 from the posts of president of the former Supreme Court and president of the National Council of Justice violated his rights of access to a court and freedom of expression. The ECHR stated that the premature termination of the applicant's mandate as president of the Supreme Court was not reviewed, nor was it open to review, by an ordinary tribunal or other body exercising judicial powers. According to the ECHR, this lack of judicial review was the result of legislation whose compatibility with the requirements of the rule of law was doubtful. The ECHR also concluded that the premature termination of his mandate was prompted by views and criticisms that he had publicly expressed in his professional capacity concerning the acts passed after 2010 that affected the judicial system. The ECHR noted that it was not only his right but also his duty as president of the National Council of Justice to express his opinion on legislative reforms affecting the judiciary.

In December 2015 the International Bar Association's Human Rights Institute (IBAHRI) released a report that concluded the independence of the judiciary and the rule of law were under threat. The IBAHRI report sharply criticized the nomination procedure for Constitutional Court justices and the reduced authority of the Constitutional Court. IBAHRI also concluded that the functions of the National Judicial Council were insufficient to oversee the activities of the president of the NOJ. IBAHRI expressed concern that the council was too weak to function as an independent body for judicial self-regulation as intended and that the Constitutional Court's ability to protect the rights guaranteed by the constitution was restricted. IBAHRI also found the ombudsman interpreted the office's mandate too narrowly when seeking to bring cases before the Constitutional Court. The Ministry of Justice rejected IBAHRI's criticisms and asserted that the legal framework provided sufficient protections against potential direct or indirect governmental interference in the operation of the judiciary. On October 5, the Human Rights Council of the United Nations General Assembly formally adopted the Universal Periodic Review of Hungary, which included a recommendation that the government should implement reforms on judicial independence and rule of law recommended by the IBAHRI in 2015.

Government officials at times gave statements in their official capacities that were widely seen as attempts to influence judicial decisions and challenge the concept of judicial independence. In one example, on January 28, Bence Tuzson, state secretary for government communication of the prime minister's cabinet office, publicly criticized a ruling of the Veszprem Tribunal, stating "the cabinet finds it outrageous that no one is held responsible for a case of such weight as the toxic sludge disaster, which claimed 10 human lives" in 2010. Tuzson stated that the cabinet "strongly urges" authorities to appeal the verdict because "the truth shall be revealed." On January 31, vice president and deputy faction leader of Fidesz, Szilard Nemeth, announced that Fidesz was initiating a debate in the Justice Committee of parliament in connection with the toxic red sludge case and a high-profile misappropriation case involving the former Socialist deputy mayor of Budapest. Nemeth asserted that ordinary people were "justifiably outraged" by both verdicts and called the independence of judges a "liberal requirement." No such meeting had taken place at the Judiciary Committee as of the end of November. On February 1, Peter Darak, president of the Curia, stated that "judicial judgement free from all external influence is under absolute constitutional protection, therefore statements suggesting contrary expectations undermine the foundation of a state governed by the rule of law." He added that it was particularly important that the other branches of government refrain from such statements. On February 2, Tunde Hando, president of NOJ, also urged representatives of the other branches of power to respect the independence of judges.

During the year Transparency International Hungary (TI-H) repeated concerns expressed by the European Commission for Democracy through Law (Venice Commission) in 2012 in connection with "the high level of independence of the prosecutor general, which is reinforced by his or her strong hierarchical control over all other prosecutors." TI-H criticized the right of the prosecutor general to give instructions to subordinate prosecutors in individual cases, to take over any case from any prosecutor, and to reassign cases to different prosecutors at any stage of the procedure without providing any reasoning. In addition, TI-H criticized the lack of an independent forum where decisions by prosecutors not to bring cases to court may be challenged. In July 2015 the Group of States against Corruption (GRECO) of the Council of Europe released a report expressing concern that the prosecutor general may remain in office indefinitely after the expiration of his or her nine-year term until parliament elects a successor by a two-thirds majority vote. According to GRECO, this procedure considerably increased the influence of politics in the selection of a prosecutor general (see section 4).

Trial Procedures

The constitution and law provide for the right to a fair public trial, and an independent judiciary generally enforced this right.

Defendants are presumed innocent until proven guilty. Suspects have the right to be informed promptly of the nature of charges against them and of the applicable legal regulations, with free interpretation as necessary. Trial proceedings are public, although a judge may minimize public attendance and may order closed hearings under certain conditions. Trials generally occurred without undue delay. Defendants have the right to be present at their trial. Immediately after defendants are informed of the charges against them, they must be advised of their right to choose a defense counsel or to request the appointment of one. If the participation of the defense counsel is mandatory in the procedure, defendants must be informed that, unless they retain defense counsel within 72 hours, the prosecutor or the investigating authority will appoint counsel for them at public expense. If a defendant declares that he or she does not wish to retain counsel, the prosecutor or the investigating authority appoints counsel immediately.

The law stipulates that the investigating authority shall schedule the time of the interrogation in a way that enables defendants to exercise their right to a defense. In the trial phase, a summons for the court hearing must be delivered at least five days prior to the hearing. Defendants have the right to free interpretation as necessary from the moment charged through all appeals. During trial, defendants and their legal counsel have complete access to evidence held by the prosecution that is relevant to their cases. Defendants may challenge or question witnesses and present witnesses and evidence on their own behalf. The law states that no one may be compelled to provide self-incriminating testimony or produce self-incriminating evidence. Defendants have the right of appeal. These rights were extended to all citizens.

Human rights NGOs continued to criticize the legal measures available to authorities to prosecute and incarcerate juveniles under certain circumstances. The criminal code sets 12 as the minimum age at which authorities may prosecute juveniles for homicide, voluntary manslaughter, grievous assault, robbery, or plundering, but only if at the time of committing the criminal offense they had the capacity to understand its consequences. Under the rules, courts may not impose prison sentences on juveniles that were between the ages of 12 and 14 when allegedly committing the criminal offense, but they may order special measures, such as placement in a juvenile correctional institute. Pretrial detention for juveniles between the ages of 12 and 14 may not last more than one year and it is to take place in a juvenile correctional institute. For juveniles over the age of 14, the maximum length of detention is two years, and they may be placed in a juvenile correctional institute or penitentiary upon court decision. The law on petty offenses permits courts to incarcerate juveniles for up to 45 days; unpaid fines may also result in confinement. Rules on community service apply only to juveniles over the age of 16.

Political Prisoners and Detainees

There were no reports of political prisoners or detainees.

Civil Judicial Procedures and Remedies

By law, individuals or organizations may seek civil remedies for human rights violations through domestic courts. Individuals or organizations who have exhausted domestic legal remedies regarding violations of the European Convention on Human Rights allegedly committed by the state may appeal to the ECHR for redress.

f. Arbitrary or Unlawful Interference with Privacy, Family, Home, or Correspondence

The constitution and law prohibit such actions, and there were no reports the government failed to respect these prohibitions.

There is no requirement for prior judicial authorization of surveillance by TEK and sometimes by the national intelligence services in cases related to national security that involve prevention of terrorism or are related to rescuing citizens captured abroad in conflict zones or by terrorist groups. In such cases, the minister of justice (instead of a judge) issues a permit for the covert intelligence action for 90 days, with a possibility of extension. Such intelligence collection may involve secret house searches, surveillance with recording devices, opening of letters and parcels, and checking and recording electronic or computerized communications without the consent of the persons under investigation. This decision is not subject to appeal.

On January 12, the ECHR ruled (effective as of June 6) that the law authorizing the surveillance of citizens by law enforcement bodies without court approval constitutes a violation of the right to privacy. The ECHR found that the scope of the measures could allow them to be applied to virtually anyone; that the authorization of surveillance takes place entirely within the executive and without an assessment of strict necessity; that new technologies enable the government to intercept masses of data concerning persons outside the original range of operation; and that effective remedial measures are absent. Prior to the ECHR verdict, a 2013 ruling of the Constitutional Court established that external control over any surveillance authorized by the minister was effectively exercised by parliament's National Security Committee and the ombudsman. Parliament did not amend the law to introduce general mandatory judiciary approval to authorize secret surveillance during the year. On June 7, parliament amended the law to include digital communication service providers among the companies obligated to store and turn over metadata and communication content, except end-to-end encryption, to police, the TEK, intelligence services, and criminal investigators of the tax authority.

The City Is for All (AVM), a grassroots organization advocating for the rights of homeless persons, continued to report that police engaged in wide-ranging discrimination against the approximately 30,000 homeless persons in the country, one-third of whom lived in the capital. In March 2015 the AVM and the HHC jointly filed a case with the Equal Treatment Authority (ETA) alleging that police conducted excessive identification checks on homeless persons during a year-long participatory action research project by the AVM in 2014. On January 15, ETA concluded a formal agreement between the HHC and the Budapest Police Headquarters (BRFK). Based on this agreement, the BRFK issued a circular note on May 10 instructing Budapest police that identification checks are to be strictly purpose-limited proceedings prompted by specific circumstances and not subject persons to identity checks merely on the basis of the physical appearance of homelessness. Police also introduced the circular note in the training curricula of the most affected police officers. According to the AVM, the police circular note failed to reduce discriminatory police actions against homeless people effectively.

Section 2. Respect for Civil Liberties, Including:

a. Freedom of Speech and Press

The constitution and the law provide for freedom of speech and press. The broad powers of the media regulatory authority, however, together with a high level of media concentration and an advertising market highly dependent on governmental contracts maintained a climate conducive to self-censorship and political influence. The Hungarian Civil Liberties Union (HCLU) continued to report bias in news reporting by the public media.

<u>Freedom of Speech and Expression</u>: The law prohibits the incitement of hatred against members of certain groups. Any person who publicly incites hatred against any national, ethnic, racial, or religious group or certain other designated groups of

the population may be prosecuted and convicted of a felony punishable by imprisonment for up to three years. The constitution includes hate speech provisions to "protect the dignity of the Hungarian nation or of any national, ethnic, racial, or religious community." The provisions provide for judicial remedies for damage to individuals and their communities that result from hate speech. In 2013 the Venice Commission raised concern that the "dignity of the Hungarian nation" provision could be applied to curtail criticism of the country's institutions and office holders, which would be incompatible with the standards of free speech limitations in a democratic society.

On May 17, the Media Council issued a resolution in connection with an article by Zsolt Bayer published in both the print and online platforms of *Magyar Hirlap* in November 2015. The Media Council ruled that Magyar Hirlap Publishing Kft. violated the legal ban on inciting hatred against and promoting exclusion of peoples, nations, national, ethnic, linguistic and other minorities, or any majority or religious community. Consequently, the Media Council ordered the immediate removal of the contested op-ed from the website of *Magyar Hirlap*; imposed a fine of 250,000 forints ($895) on the publisher; and ordered the publication of a statement on the homepage of *Magyar Hirlap* for one week. The statement included the Media Council resolution and noted that the "author described the community of migrants as a homogenous group being in war with European societies, calling every member of this community above the age of 14 potential murderers." On August 18, Zsolt Bayer received a state award (Knight's Cross of the Hungarian Order of Merit) from the minister of the Prime Minister's Office (see also section 6, Anti-Semitism).

The law prohibits public denial of, expression of, doubt about, or minimization of the Holocaust, genocide, and other crimes of the National Socialist (Nazi) and communist regimes, which are punishable by a maximum sentence of three years in prison.

Through the end of October, the Action and Protection Foundation (TEV) reported nine cases of Holocaust denial, of which four were pending, three were suspended, one was rejected by police, and one was closed.

On June 1, the Buda Central District Court ordered the temporary removal from the internet of nearly 20 websites for violating the legal ban of Holocaust denial. The prosecutor's office argued that the websites were promoting and selling the Hungarian translation of a book by a Swedish author claiming that Nazi regimes did not commit genocide.

The law prohibits as a petty offense the wearing, exhibiting, or promoting of the swastika, the logo of the Nazi SS, the symbols of the arrow cross, the hammer and sickle, or the five-pointed red star in a way that harms human dignity or the memory of the victims of dictatorships.

On May 16, the ECHR ruled that freedom of expression of seven opposition members of parliament was violated in 2013, when parliamentary speaker Kover fined them for alleged "seriously disruptive conduct considered gravely offensive to parliamentary order." The members had displayed a large placard and banners in the parliamentary chamber, and one used a megaphone to speak during the course of a vote. The ECHR found that the interference with the members' right to freedom of expression was not "necessary in a democratic society." The ECHR also found a lack of procedural safeguards because the members had no remedy under domestic law to contest the disciplinary decisions imposed on them. Nevertheless, the ECHR acknowledged that a 2014 amendment to the law introduced minimum procedural safeguards by providing the possibility for a member of parliament who had been fined to make representations before a parliamentary committee.

On January 21, the Buda Central District Court acquitted the man who kicked a polystyrene head of Prime Minister Viktor Orban at an antigovernment demonstration in 2013. The man was charged with committing a rowdy act, but he stated it was an expression of political opinion. The prosecutor appealed the verdict but the Budapest Metropolitan Court upheld it in a legally binding ruling on November 24.

Press and Media Freedoms: A massive reshuffling in the media market that started in 2015 continued during the year, resulting in further expansion of government-friendly enterprises and reduction in independent media voices in television, radio, print, and online media through the launching of new media outlets, acquisitions of existing outlets, efforts to further bolster state media, and the sudden closure of the country's largest independent daily newspaper. The state media continued to be the frequent object of criticism that its coverage of news reflected the government's views and that it concealed unfavorable facts and opinions.

Under the legal framework for the media sector, the National Media and Infocommunications Authority (NMHH), subordinate to parliament, is the central state administrative body for regulating the media. The authority of NMHH includes overseeing the operation of broadcast and media markets as well as "contributing to the execution of the government's policy in the areas of frequency management and telecommunications." The NMHH president also serves as the chair of the five-member Media Council, which is the decision making body of the NMHH and supervises broadcast, cable, online, and print media content and spectrum management. Human rights NGOs remained highly critical of the NMHH for being a politically homogeneous body consisting of members nominated exclusively by the governing parties and of the law governing the media for failing to secure media pluralism and the independence of public-service media.

A 2015 report of the Venice Commission on the media laws noted that media content restrictions were unclear and allowed for an excessively broad interpretation by the courts. It also found fault with restrictions on criticism of religious or political views and stipulations that media content cannot violate privacy rights. The report criticized the composition of the Media Council and procedures for selecting its head as failing to ensure independence and political neutrality and lacking diverse representation of relevant media stakeholders. The report also noted that the public media was overly centralized and that content was supplied nearly exclusively by the government-controlled National News Agency (MTI).

On April 26, parliamentary speaker Laszlo Kover banned journalists representing *Nepszabadsag*, *HVG*, *24.hu*, and *Index* from parliament for an indefinite period, one day after he was filmed ignoring their questions about possible corruption related to the Hungarian National Bank. Kover asserted that the reporters had been working in areas of the building that were off limits to the media, based on a previous order of the speaker. As of September 12, Kover suspended the ban. On October 20, Kover banned all employees of the news website *444.hu* indefinitely after reporters momentarily blocked the path of the Fidesz faction spokesperson while asking questions about a high-level government official's use of a helicopter to attend a wedding (see also section 3, Elections and Political Participation, and section 4).

On October 8, the operations of the country's largest independent daily newspaper, *Nepszabadsag*, were suddenly suspended by its parent company. Prior to the suspension, employees had been told to pack their effects to move to new office space, but when they arrived on October 8 they were informed of the newspaper's closure and denied access to company offices. Both the print and online versions ceased operations, and *Nepszabadsag's* website, including its archive of past news stories, was made unavailable. The newspaper's management company, the

Austrian-based Mediaworks, stated the suspension was an economic decision because the newspaper had been losing readership and money and would continue until the company found a new business model. Some employees and media watchers noted that *Nepszabadsag* had turned a profit in 2015, as had Mediaworks itself. Some employees and government critics linked the sudden closure to *Nepszabadsag's* exposes of government corruption, including a cabinet minister's use of a helicopter to attend a celebrity wedding and nepotism involving the girlfriend of the national bank president.

Several domestic and foreign media outlets expressed solidarity with *Nepszabadsag* journalists and several thousand persons demonstrated in front of parliament against shutting the daily on the evening of October 8. The European Commission spokesperson stated the EC was following the situation closely and was "very concerned" about the shutting of the newspaper. The European Journalists Federation expressed dismay at the closure of *Nepszabadsag*, calling the termination of the daily a serious blow to media pluralism. OSCE media representative Dunja Mijatovic also described the closure as a huge blow to freedom of the press and media diversity. The government echoed Mediaworks' statement that the closure was an economic decision, adding that it would be a violation of the freedom of the press for it to intervene.

Violence and Harassment: On April 14, the European Center for Press and Media Freedom (ECPMF) sent a letter to the prime minister asking him to initiate an investigation into the assault by police on journalists and camera crews from Serbia, Slovakia, and Australia while they were covering the attempt by hundreds of asylum seekers to get through the border fence in September 2015 and the consequent response by border guards. The ECPMF called it "unacceptable" that, instead of investigating the assault on foreign journalists, the government declared the police action lawful and professional and blamed the victims for not leaving the country where the police had been using coercive measures. The ECPMF also found it "worrisome" that the state media covered the incident and the refugee crisis more generally in a biased, unbalanced way. On May 23, Minister of Interior Sandor Pinter responded to the ECPMF letter, rejecting reports that police beat and arrested foreign journalists. In November 2015, upon the report of the HHC, the Szeged department of the Central Investigative Prosecutor's Office launched an investigation against unknown perpetrators for mistreatment during official proceedings in connection with the incident. The investigation remained pending.

Censorship or Content Restrictions: The law provides content regulations and standards for journalistic rights, ethics, and norms that are applicable to all media, including news portals and online publications. It prohibits inciting hatred against nations; communities; ethnic, linguistic, or other minorities; majority groups; and churches or religious groups. It provides for maintaining the confidentiality of sources with respect to procedures conducted by courts or authorities.

The Media Council may impose fines for violations of content regulations, including on media services that violate prohibitions on inciting hatred or violating human dignity or regulations governing the protection of minors. The council may impose fines of up to 200 million forints ($717,000), depending on the nature of the infringement, type of media service, and audience size. It may also suspend the right to broadcast for up to one week. Defendants may appeal Media Council decisions but must appeal separately to prevent implementation of fines while the parties litigate the substantive appeal. As of August 1, the Media Council issued 106 resolutions imposing fines totaling 31.5 million forints ($113,000) on 61 media outlets. Twelve defendants challenged those resolutions in court.

On May 9, Mertek Standard Media Monitor released its annual report, *The Methods are Old, the Cronies are New--Soft Censorship in the Hungarian Media in 2015*. The report cited "the market expansion of the pro-Fidesz interests at every level of the value chain, be it through a politically biased distribution of radio frequencies or the manipulative allocation of state advertisements." Concerning state media, the report highlighted the market-distorting impact of nontransparent and excessive funding as well as the documented practice of concealment of news or certain viewpoints and even the doctoring of some news items to serve the government's needs. Based on interviews with media executives, the report concluded that statutory rules and the institutional framework governing the operations of media are not the main impediments to press freedom. It found instead that "the dearth of funding makes media vulnerable and potentially leads them to compromise their principles, while the lack of equipment and staff also constitute serious challenges to quality journalism and investigative reporting."

On May 2, Janos Karpati, former MTI correspondent in Brussels, stated at a conference that those working at state-run radio, television, and the MTI were advised to consult their superiors about what questions they could ask members of the cabinet. Karpati, who had been working for MTI since 1981 until he was dismissed earlier in the year, further stated, "questions arrive from up above to the editor and the correspondent" with instructions such as "emphasize this; ask this; or do not ask that."

<u>Libel/Slander Laws</u>: Individuals may be sued for libel for their published statements or for publicizing libelous statements made by others. Plaintiffs may litigate in both civil and criminal courts. Journalists reporting on an event may be judged criminally responsible for making or reporting false statements.

The HCLU reported that public officials, especially in small towns, continued to use libel and defamation laws to silence criticisms from citizens and journalists. According to the HCLU, there were several dozen cases per year in which public officials pursued both criminal and civil charges (often simultaneously) against individuals for expressing criticism of officials or their policies.

Internet Freedom

The government did not restrict or disrupt access to the internet or censor online content, and there were no credible reports that the government monitored private online communications without appropriate legal authority.

According to the International Telecommunication Union, approximately 72.8 percent of the population used the internet in 2015. Freedom House maintained the country's internet and digital media rating as "free."

On February 2, the ECHR found that domestic court rulings had violated the right to free expression of the Association of Hungarian Content Providers and *Index.hu Zrt*. In the rulings in question, domestic courts had found the two aggrieved parties liable for "disseminating" offensive and vulgar third-party comments that were posted on the two parties' websites. Although the two parties had immediately removed the comments from their websites when they were notified of the civil proceedings, domestic courts held they were liable for having provided space for injurious and degrading comments. In its ruling, the ECHR found that comments in response to an online article could be regarded a matter of public interest and did not amount to hate speech or incitement to violence. The ECHR established that court findings of liability in such cases may have, directly or indirectly, a chilling effect on freedom of expression on the internet.

Academic Freedom and Cultural Events

There were no government restrictions on academic freedom or cultural events.

b. Freedom of Peaceful Assembly and Association

Freedom of Assembly

The constitution and law provide for freedom of peaceful assembly, and the government generally respected this right. By law, demonstrations do not require a police permit, but event organizers must inform police of a planned assembly in a public place at least three days in advance. The law authorizes police to prohibit any gathering if it seriously endangers the peaceful operation of representative bodies or courts or if it is not possible to provide for alternate routes for traffic. Police may not disband a spontaneous, unauthorized assembly that remains peaceful and is aimed at expressing opinion on an event that was unforeseeable, but organizers must inform police without delay after the organizing has begun. Police are required to disband an assembly if it commits a crime or incites the commission of a crime, results in the violation of the rights of others, involves armed participants, or is held despite a preliminary official ban. A police decision to prohibit or disband a public demonstration is open for judicial review.

On June 6, parliament amended the law to introduce new police measures in case of a terrorist attack or the preparation of such, including the right to disband public events in the geographic area affected by the terrorist act. The police can order such special security measures for 72 hours, which can doubled if deemed necessary. The national police chief can decide on the further extension of the measure if it is justified by concrete and verified new information. The minister of interior is responsible for informing parliament's relevant committees on the extension of the security measures and for providing the relevant information used as the basis for the decision.

Through the end of September, police prohibited seven demonstrations, which constituted 0.8 percent of total announced demonstrations. Organizers requested judicial review of four demonstration requests rejected by police, and courts ultimately permitted the demonstration in one case.

NGOs continued to criticize shortcomings in the law that resulted in inconsistent police practices and court decisions with regard to both prohibiting and disbanding demonstrations.

On July 12, the Constitutional Court rejected the complaint of a petitioner concerning the police banning of a planned protest in 2014. The applicant wished to stage demonstrations at several locations on one day but police banned gatherings at three sites, including the prime minister's residence. The applicant filed a legal challenge to the ban, but the Budapest Metropolitan Administrative and Labor Court rejected it on the basis of protecting the right to privacy. The Constitutional Court found that, because the demonstration organizer could have protested at other, nonrestricted locations, the right to peaceful assembly was not disproportionately curtailed. The Constitutional Court called on parliament to amend the relevant legislation by the end of the year to resolve the conflict between the basic rights to privacy and assembly. The applicant appealed to the ECHR; that appeal remained pending. The HCLU harshly criticized the Constitutional Court ruling on the grounds that the law clearly stipulates how others' rights (e.g., right to privacy) can be protected from an assembly and therefore no further restrictions are necessary, especially in the phase of planning and organizing a demonstration. According to the HCLU, the new restriction on freedom of assembly that the Constitutional Court considers necessary would provide too broad discretion for law enforcement agencies in making unilateral decisions curtailing freedom of assembly. Despite the Constitutional Court order, parliament failed to amend the legislation on freedom of assembly by the end of the year.

On July 23, police banned a demonstration of 100 individuals planned by Zoltan Buki of the Facebook group For a Democratic Hungary for July 24 at the prime minister's residence. Police based their decision on protection of the privacy rights of the residents of the area. Buki appealed the police ban at the Budapest Metropolitan Administrative and Labor Court, which upheld the police decision on July 28. In response, on the same day, Buki announced another demonstration at the same location for July 31, but promised to keep the gathering under 50 participants, who would remain silent and only hold banners to express their opinions. On July 30, police again prohibited the demonstration attempt, but a subsequent ruling of the Budapest Metropolitan Administrative and Labor Court permitted it on August 3. On August 7, 15 persons finally held a demonstration in front of the prime minister's residence.

Freedom of Association

The constitution and the law provide for freedom of association and the government generally respected it.

c. Freedom of Religion

See the Department of State's *International Religious Freedom Report* at www.state.gov/religiousfreedomreport/.

d. Freedom of Movement, Internally Displaced Persons, Protection of Refugees, and Stateless Persons

The constitution and law provide for freedom of internal movement, foreign travel, emigration, and repatriation, and the government generally respected these rights.

<u>Abuse of Migrants, Refugees, and Stateless Persons</u>: On June 4, UNHCR announced allegations in more than 100 cases of excessive use of force and abuse against asylum seekers and migrants by border authorities aimed at preventing their irregular border crossing (crossing the border illegally). The cases included that of a 22-year-old Syrian man, who drowned in the Tisza River on June 1 when he was allegedly pushed back by "uniformed personnel" to prevent his irregular crossing from Serbia. The HHC also repeatedly expressed "extreme concerns over the unprecedented and systematic allegations of brutality and mistreatment committed by uniformed personnel on the Serbian-Hungarian border" (also see section 1.b.).

On June 13, parliament amended the law to authorize police, effective July 5, to escort irregular migrant asylum seekers apprehended within five miles of the border back to the external side of the border fence, which remains on Hungarian territory (the fence was placed six feet back from the actual border). Authorities reportedly did not register such irregular migrants but directed them, once across the fence, to proceed to the nearest of four official transit zones to submit asylum claims. UNHCR, the HHC, and Doctors without Borders (MSF) expressed concern that those pushed back were stranded for several days or weeks in inhumane conditions on the Serbian side of the border, waiting in front of the transit zones to be able to submit their asylum claim.

On July 13, HRW released a report claiming that "people who cross into Hungary without permission, including women and children, have been viciously beaten and forced back across the border." It included witness accounts of and evidence of injury from, beatings, pepper spray, and dog attacks. On July 22, MSF reported treating on the Serbian side of the border fence an increasing number of patients who "showed physical trauma directly associated with violence." Some HRW interviewees reported that they were beaten and abused by personnel wearing uniforms consistent with those of police and the military. HRW obtained photographic evidence of fresh injuries and observed bruises from injuries more than two weeks after they occurred. On July 15, UNHCR in a press statement described "dire" conditions for those--including women and children--waiting near transit zones on the Hungary-Serbia border. It also expressed deep concern over the new Hungarian border crossing restrictions that led to push-backs to Serbia of persons seeking asylum as well as over reports of violence and abuse. UNHCR asserted that the new restrictions were at variance with EU and international law. On September 27, Amnesty International (AI) released a report mirroring the earlier HRW report and UNHCR statement, criticizing reported abuse, violent push-backs across the border fence, failure to provide timely access to asylum procedures, and failure to provide adequate resources and services for migrants waiting at the border. In a press release at the time of the report, AI asserted that the "appalling treatment and labyrinthine asylum procedures are a cynical ploy to deter asylum seekers from Hungary's ever more militarized borders."

On July 13, following a visit to the Kormend refugee camp, Socialist Member of Parliament Agnes Kunhalmi stated that conditions in the camp were "squalid." Kunhamli stated that migrants in the camp did not have access to hot water and that the provided tents and food did not meet basic standards.

Between April 8 and July 5 (when the new law entered into effect), authorities prevented 22,127 irregular migrants from entering the country, and 6,859 persons between July 5 and October 18. From July 5 to October 18, authorities returned 5,493 irregular migrants to the Serbian side but none to the Croatian side of the border. By December 16, the HHC registered 409 allegations of mistreatment reported to or recorded by the HHC pertaining to the measures to maintain order on the state borders. The government publicly rejected NGO and UNHCR allegations of abuse by law enforcement officials against migrants. According to the Office of the Prosecutor General, however, 18 investigations were launched for mistreatment in official proceedings (including six upon the reports of victims) as of October in connection with police border protection measures along the Serbian border. Of the 18 investigations, the Szeged department of the Central Investigative Prosecutor's Office terminated the investigation in five cases, suspended the investigation in one case, and pressed charges in two cases. Ten investigations remained pending at the end September.

The government failed to cooperate fully with UNHCR and other humanitarian organizations in providing protection and assistance to refugees, returning refugees, asylum seekers, and stateless persons.

Protection of Refugees

As of October 18, police registered 18,006 "illegal migrants" (persons crossing the border not at the official border stations but illegally through the "green border") arriving in Hungary, compared with 391,384 in 2015. As of November 9, the Office of Immigration and Nationality (BAH) registered 28,320 asylum claims, compared with 177,135 in 2015. As of October 18, the BAH terminated more than 47,210 cases (including many launched in 2015), mainly due to the absence of the applicant (compared with 152,260 in 2015) and issued decisions on the merits in 3,706 cases (3,819 in 2015). The BAH granted refugee status, subsidiary protection, or tolerated status in 389 cases (compared with 508 in 2015), which was 11 percent of the cases assessed on the merits (13 percent in 2015).

Access to Asylum: A law adopted in 2015 with new provisions added during the year provides for the granting of refugee status, but the new system failed to provide full protection to refugees, according to UNCHR. The new system was based on enhanced physical border protection aimed at eliminating unauthorized border crossings and significantly reducing migrants' access to asylum proceeding.

In the second half of 2015, the government installed a 13-foot-high "temporary border control fence" to stop migrants and asylum seekers from unauthorized border crossing from Serbia and Croatia. The 2015 law stipulates that crossing the border illegally along the security fence at the Serbian and Croatian borders constitutes a criminal offense punishable with actual or suspended imprisonment of up to 10 years and/or expulsion. Damaging the fence or hindering its construction are also criminal offenses.

On March 9, the government announced a six-month nationwide "crisis situation prompted by mass migration," which was extended for another six months, effective from September 8. Under the special legal situation, the law authorizes the armed forces, beginning in September 2015, to assist police in maintaining order at the country's borders, explicitly including through use of instruments of coercion suitable for causing physical injury, but only with nonlethal intent. In such circumstances, soldiers receive police power (they may ask for identification, capture and detain individuals, examine clothing, packages, and vehicles, and take measures against foreigners) and may use firearms if not directed at killing others (see also section 1.d., Role of the Police and Security Apparatus).

Effective from July 5, the law authorizes police to escort irregular migrants apprehended within five miles of the border back to the external side of the border fence, which remains Hungarian territory. In such cases, authorities reportedly did not register irregular migrants or allow them to submit an asylum claim, although they provided migrants information on how to proceed to the nearest official transit zone if they wished to submit an asylum claim. Given that the country only accepted a limited number of asylum applications a day at these transit zones, those pushed outside were unable to pursue an asylum claim sometimes for weeks. In effect, authorities pushed potential asylum seekers back to Serbia without providing them an opportunity to seek protection in the country except after long delay. International and domestic organizations reported broad allegations of mistreatment by authorities during push-back procedures (see Abuse of Migrants, Refugees, and Stateless Persons).

In September and October 2015, the government opened four official "transit zones" for administering asylum applications along the border with Serbia and Croatia (in Roszke, Tompa, Beremend, and Letenye). The original capacity of each transit zone was 100 applicants per day, which was reduced to 15 per day per transit zone on March 22 and further reduced to 10 per day on November 2. These transit zones, operated by the BAH, are responsible for assessing the eligibility of the asylum applicants based on safe country of origin and safe third-country provisions and transferring eligible cases to an assessment proceeding within eight days. The rules exempt "asylum seekers with special needs" (such as unaccompanied minors, the elderly, persons with disabilities, pregnant women, single parents with children, and victims of torture) from the admissibility border procedure, and such applicants immediately enter the assessment phase of the asylum process, at which point their applications are reviewed on their merits. Once the application enters the assessment phase, the applicant is permitted to enter the country's territory and becomes eligible for government services provided to asylum seekers. If the BAH rejects the application in the assessment phase, the applicant is immediately issued an order of expulsion but has seven days to appeal the decision in court, where judges or court clerks issue a legally binding ruling in eight days. Courts may quash administrative decisions and refer applicants back to the BAH for a new procedure but have no authority to change the decision on the asylum application.

On May 12, UNHCR released a report concluding that the 2015 and 2016 laws and practice "have had the combined effect of limiting and deterring access to asylum in the country" and raised "serious concerns as regards compatibility with international and European law." According to UNHCR, the asylum procedure and reception conditions in the transit zones were not in accordance with EU and international standards, in particular concerning procedural safeguards, judicial review, and freedom of movement.

On July 15, the HHC released a report criticizing the authorization of automatic push-back of persons potentially in need of international protection over the fence to the border area of Hungary and Serbia. Reports suggested that push-backs also occur from deep within the territory of the country. The HHC report concluded that "legalizing push-backs from deep within Hungarian territory denies asylum seekers the right to seek international protection, in breach of international and EU law."

The infringement procedure launched by the European Commission in December 2015 against the country in connection with asylum regulations remained pending at the end of the year. The European Commission raised specific concerns regarding the lack of interpretation and translation in the context of fast-tracked criminal proceedings for irregular border crossers; the lack of possibility to refer to new facts and circumstances during the asylum procedure; the lack of automatic suspension of expulsion orders in case of appeals; the possibility to reject an asylum application without a personal hearing; and the issuance of decisions by court secretaries (a sub-judicial level) who lack judicial independence.

Safe Country of Origin/Transit: In July 2015 the government issued lists of "safe countries of origin" and "safe third countries." Both lists included EU member and candidate states (except Turkey, but including Serbia), member states of the European Economic Area, Bosnia and Herzegovina, Kosovo, Switzerland, Canada, Australia, New Zealand, and those states of the United States of America that do not apply the death penalty. On March 31, the government updated the list of safe third countries to include Turkey. UNHCR and the HHC repeatedly noted their objection to the government's recognition of Serbia as a safe transit country.

As of November 9, the BAH rejected 2,036 asylum applications based on inadmissibility due to safe country of origin and safe third-country provisions (7 percent of all applications). Upon appeal, the BAH did not change any original decisions of inadmissibility.

Refoulement: The government did not send asylum seekers back to conflict zones where their lives or freedom would be at risk. UNHCR and the HHC, however, criticized the government for issuing inadmissibility decisions based on Serbia being considered as a safe third country. According to UNHCR, Serbia lacked a functioning asylum system, thus the return of asylum seekers to Serbia may result in their exposure to inhuman treatment and refoulement to other unsafe countries. As of September 2015, however, Serbia refused to take back asylum seekers unless they were Serbian, Albanian, or Kosovar citizens or other individuals holding valid travel and/or entry documents.

<u>Freedom of movement</u>: The law permits detention of asylum seekers under certain circumstances. The law requires that detention of asylum seekers be based on an individual assessment and only occur absent alternative means to provide for the presence of the applicant at asylum proceedings. Judges must decide every 60 days whether to extend a decision to keep an illegal migrant in custody. The law provides that detention of asylum seekers may not exceed six months, or 30 days in case of families with children. Unaccompanied minors are exempted from asylum detention, and alternatives to detention (such as bail) must also be considered before ordering detention. On November 21, 330 asylum applicants were in asylum detention. As of November 9, 2,363 asylum seekers (eight percent of all asylum applicants) were in asylum detention.

On July 5, the ECHR ruled that the "asylum detention" of a gay Iranian asylum seeker was arbitrary and therefore unlawful. The ECHR found that authorities failed to make an individualized assessment and take into account the applicant's vulnerability in the detention facility, based on his sexual orientation. The ECHR emphasized that authorities should exercise special care when deciding on deprivation of liberty in order to avoid situations that may reproduce the conditions that forced asylum seekers to flee in the first place.

The law provides that irregular migrants in an expulsion procedure (including rejected asylum seekers) can be placed in "immigration detention," which may not exceed 12 months or 30 days for families with children. Unaccompanied minors are exempted from immigration detention. Immigration detention is subject to periodic judicial review. The regulations effective from September 2015 make the acts of crossing the border illegally through the security fence, damaging the fence, or hindering the construction of the fence punishable by imprisonment. Authorities usually put convicted illegal border crossers in immigration detention in preparation for their expulsion. As of November 21, authorities kept 138 irregular migrants in immigration detention (see also section 1.d., Protracted Detention of Asylum Seekers or Stateless Persons).

On November 3, the CPT released a report on its ad hoc visit in October 2015 aimed at examining the treatment and conditions of detention of foreign nationals as well as legal safeguards offered to them. The CPT report raised concerns regarding criminal investigations pursued against foreign nationals who had irregularly crossed a border fence, even if they had submitted an application for international protection. The report recalled the 1951 Geneva Convention of the Status of Refugees, which stipulates that contracting states "shall not impose penalties, on account of their illegal entry or presence, on refugees who, coming directly from a territory where their life or freedom was threatened, enter or are present in their territory without authorization, provided they present themselves without delay to the authorities and show good cause for their illegal entry or presence." The CPT report asserted that this provision applies to "persons who have briefly transited other countries or who are unable to find effective protection in the first country or countries to which they flee." On November 3, the government officially responded to the report, stating its view that the 1951 Convention delineated a prohibition of "imposing a penalty" and not a prohibition on launching "criminal proceedings" against refugees who enter or are present in the country without authorization. According to the government's response, domestic law stipulates the exclusion or the limitation of criminal culpability or the punishability in cases defined by the convention. On November 4, the HHC released a statement asserting that, contrary to the government's position, domestic law failed to unequivocally exclude or limit criminal culpability in cases of irregular border crossing by asylum seekers, which resulted in repeated court convictions in such cases.

Between September 2015 and November 30, some 2,895 persons faced criminal trial for offenses related to the border fence, of whom 2,843 were convicted for the "prohibited crossing of the border closure."

On March 22, the HHC, together with the Cordelia Foundation, the Foundation for Access to Rights, and the Assistance Center for Torture Survivors, released a report, *From Torture to Detention*. The report criticized the lack of systematic identification mechanisms to prevent the detention of torture victims and other traumatized asylum seekers; the presence of numerous factors that could lead to retraumatization in detention, including the lack of proper information; lack of access to interpretation in crucial situations; unnecessary limitations on contact with the outside world and on internal freedom of movement; and the lack of specialized medical and psychological and psychosocial care.

UNHCR expressed concerns over the number of persons kept in detention while awaiting expulsion to Serbia.

The November 3 CPT report stated that a "considerable number of foreign nationals claimed that they had been subjected to physical mistreatment by police officers." The allegations concerned mainly slaps and punches to the face or abdomen as well as baton blows at the moment of apprehension, even when the persons concerned were allegedly not resisting apprehension or after they had been brought under control; during transfer to a police establishment; and/or during subsequent police questioning. Foreign nationals who claimed to be unaccompanied minors made some of these allegations. In addition, "a few allegations were received of physical mistreatment by police officers and/or armed guards working in immigration or asylum detention facilities." Moreover, some allegations were received of verbal abuse and disrespectful behavior on the part of police officers and armed guards (such as swearing, mocking, and spitting at foreign nationals); these allegations pertained to all stages of deprivation of liberty.

As of September 30, one person filed a report for mistreatment during an official procedure at the Kiskunhalas immigration detention facility. Subsequently the Military Council of the Szeged Tribunal imposed a fine of 130,000 forints ($465) and reprimanded the convicted police officer. As of September 30, six persons filed reports of mistreatment during an official procedure against police officers at the Nyirbator asylum detention facility. The Debrecen Regional Office of the Central Investigative Prosecutor's Office launched investigations in each case, which remained pending.

Access to Basic Services: On May 10, parliament amended the law to curtail measures aimed at facilitating the integration of beneficiaries of international protection on the grounds that they should not have more advantages than citizens. The new measures include the introduction of mandatory and automatic revision of refugee status at least every three years; reduction of the maximum period of stay in open reception centers after recognition from 60 to 30 days; decrease of the eligibility period for basic health care services following recognition from one year to six months; and termination of housing allowances, educational allowances, and monthly cash allowances previously provided for asylum seekers and beneficiaries of international protection or tolerated status.

Durable Solutions: The country is party to the 2013 Dublin III regulation, which provides for the return of asylum seekers to the first EU member state they entered for processing, although the government strictly limited the acceptance of Dublin III returnees during the year. As of October 31, the country accepted 452 Dublin III returnees out of 24,446 whose return was requested by other EU member states (1.9 percent).

On February 24, the government initiated a national referendum on the question, "Do you agree that the European Union should have the power to impose the compulsory settlement of non-Hungarian citizens in Hungary without the consent of the parliament of Hungary?" The government actively campaigned for voters to choose the "no" response to the referendum question. The referendum, held on

October 2, was legally invalid, as the number of votes fell short of the 50 percent threshold needed to be valid. The turnout was 43.91 percent, but only 41.07 percent in terms of unspoiled or error-free ballots. Among valid ballots, 98.32 percent supported the government-favored "no" response and only 1.68 percent responded "yes."

<u>Temporary Protection</u>: The government provided temporary protection ("subsidiary protection" and "tolerated status") to individuals who did not qualify as refugees. The law defines subsidiary protection as protection provided to foreigners who do not satisfy the criteria for recognition as a refugee but who, in the event of their return to their country of origin, would risk exposure to "serious harm." The law also provides that the BAH may authorize persons to stay in the country by granting them "tolerated status" for one year (extendable) consistent with the country's nonrefoulement obligations under international law. As of November 9, the BAH received 389 refugee claims (the majority from Afghan nationals) and granted 136 persons refugee status, 246 persons subsidiary protection status, and seven persons tolerated status.

Section 3. Freedom to Participate in the Political Process

The constitution and law provide citizens the ability to choose their government in periodic elections held by secret ballot and based on universal suffrage. OSCE election observers noted the ruling party enjoyed undue advantages, and the opposition and some civil society groups described the 2014 national elections as "free but not fair."

Elections and Political Participation

<u>Recent Elections</u>: The most recent national elections were held in 2014 under a single-round national system to elect 199 members of parliament. The elections resulted in the ruling parties gaining a second consecutive two-thirds super-majority in parliament, receiving 45 percent of party-list votes while winning 96 of the country's 106 single-member districts, allocated through a first-past-the-post system. In March 2015 the governing coalition lost its two-thirds majority in parliament following a February by-election in Veszprem.

A mission representing the OSCE Office for Democratic Institutions and Human Rights (ODIHR) observed the 2014 elections. In its final report issued in 2014, the mission concluded that, while the elections were efficiently administered and offered voters a diverse choice following an inclusive candidate registration process, "the main governing party enjoyed an undue advantage because of restrictive campaign regulations, biased media coverage, and campaign activities that blurred the separation between political party and the state."

The 2014 ODIHR election observation mission report noted that the process of redistricting constituencies was widely criticized "for lacking transparency, independence, and consultation, and allegations of gerrymandering were widespread." The report found that the practice of transferring surplus votes of constituency winners to party lists resulted in the ruling Fidesz-KDNP coalition gaining six additional seats.

<u>Political Parties and Political Participation</u>: In its 2014 report, the ODIHR observation mission reported several problems with media influence, including the increasing ownership of media outlets by businesspersons directly or indirectly associated with Fidesz and the allocation of state advertising to select media outlets. It concluded that these factors undermined the pluralism of the media and increased self-censorship among journalists. The report also criticized the use of government advertisements that were almost identical to those of Fidesz campaign ads, claiming that they contributed to an uneven playing field and did not fully respect the principle of separation of party and state. The ODIHR mission noted the limited amount of free broadcast time available for candidates and absence of paid political advertising on nationwide commercial television and concluded that this situation impeded candidates' ability to campaign via the media. The report also criticized campaign financing laws that limited the transparency and accountability of political parties and expressed concern over the lack of effective redress for complaints filed during the electoral process.

Citizens living abroad but having permanent residency in the country were required to appear in person at embassies to vote, while citizens not having domestic residency could vote by mail, but only for party lists. ODIHR election observers noted that the practice of applying different procedures to register and vote depending on whether or not a person had a permanent address in the country resulted in unequal treatment of voters outside the country. Nonetheless, in March 2015, the ECHR rejected the application of citizens living abroad but having permanent residency in the country, who objected that they were compelled to appear in person at embassies to vote, while dual citizens not having residency in the country could vote by mail. On April 19, the Constitutional Court rejected a constitutional complaint on similar grounds and concluded that the contested legal provision was not discriminatory, since those without an address in the country could only vote for party lists. TI-H and other NGOs maintained their position that the different procedures applied in case of citizens with and without permanent residency in the country severely violated the principle of providing an equal opportunity to vote.

There was one case of physical interference in an official opposition party political activity. On February 23, a group of approximately 15-20 men physically impeded Istvan Nyako, a member of the opposition Hungarian Socialist Party, from submitting a referendum request (regarding an unpopular law closing retail stores on Sundays) at the National Election Office ahead of a rival proposal by Mrs. Laszlo Erdosi, the wife of the mayor of Herceghalom. The order of submission was critical because the National Election Committee only considered the first application for a referendum, and only one proposal on a given topic was considered at a time. After a series of legal challenges, police and prosecutorial investigations, and court rulings, no charges were brought against the group of men by the end of the year. On March 3, however, the Curia established that the group impeded Nyako in exercising his right to initiate a referendum, and in a separate ruling on April 6 declared Nyako's referendum petition to be the first one officially registered, thus authorizing the request. On April 12, parliament revoked the act in question, making the referendum moot, and, on May 10, amended the law to permit competing referendum requests, setting a rule that referenda must be held on questions for which supporters first gather 200,000 signatures.

<u>Participation of Women and Minorities</u>: Representation of women in public life was very low. Women constituted 10 percent of members of parliament, and there were no female ministers. Only 13 percent of sub-cabinet-level government state secretaries were women. On May 27, the UN Working Group on the Issue of Discrimination against Women in Law and in Practice released a statement following an official visit. The report noted "pervasive and severe gender stereotyping of women which undoubtedly contributed to their low level of political participation." The UN working group expressed concerns over "some public officials who legitimize and justify the low representation of women in politics."

The electoral system provides 13 recognized national minorities the possibility of registering for a separate minority voting process in parliamentary elections. While all 13 national minorities registered candidate lists, none obtained enough votes in 2014 to win a minority seat in parliament. As a result, each nationality was represented in parliament by a nonvoting spokesperson whose competence was limited to discussing minority issues. The ODIHR report on the 2014 elections concluded that, because voters publicly register to vote for minority lists and such lists give only one choice of candidate on the ballot, their choice was limited and the secrecy of their vote was violated. Due to privacy laws regarding ethnic data, no statistics were available on the number of members of a minority who were in parliament or the cabinet.

Section 4. Corruption and Lack of Transparency in Government

The law provides criminal penalties for corruption by officials. The European Commission and NGOs contended that the government did not implement the law effectively, and officials often engaged in corrupt practices with impunity. The same observers noted that authorities were consistently reluctant to investigate corruption allegations in a transparent, public manner. There were numerous reports of government corruption during the year.

Corruption: TI-H and K-Monitor continued to report that the economy was "dominated by cronyism and state capitalism." According to these anticorruption NGOs, the situation amounted to "state capture," characterized by "the opaque symbiosis between an extensive and expansive government and powerful business groups, who may easily out-compete public interest." The NGOs reported a number of examples indicating "the government's intention to grant privileges to certain economic actors by legal means." TI-H noted that there was no designated anticorruption agency and that agencies with anticorruption duties, such as the prosecution service, the State Audit Office, police, and the tax administration, often failed to take action against corruption.

The most significant corruption case of the year was the unlawful allocation of public funds worth approximately 267 billion forints ($960 million)--equivalent to almost one percent of GDP--by the Central Bank of Hungary (MNB) to six private foundations it established in 2013 and 2014. The transfer of public assets to MNB foundations effectively deprived the parliament and ministries of fiduciary oversight and the state budget of potential resources. On March 1, parliament adopted a retroactive law to prevent the MNB foundations' expenses and operations from becoming public. After opposition parties and anticorruption watchdogs heavily criticized the bill, President Janos Ader refused to sign it and referred it to the Constitutional Court for review. On March 30, one day prior to the Constitutional Court ruling, the Curia ordered the MNB to publish data on how its six foundations spent the assets entrusted to them. The data exposed extensive conflicts of interest on MNB foundation boards, favoritism in MNB foundation investments, and possible infringement of EU monetary financing rules.

Documents released by the foundations also showed that they did not issue public tenders for purchases, as required by public procurement laws.

On March 31, the Constitutional Court ruled that the March 1 law was unconstitutional and determined that, since the MNB serves public duties and manages public funds, information on the foundations' activities must remain publicly available. On April 7, the European Central Bank warned that MNB foundation activities could potentially conflict with rules against monetary financing.

The information on MNB foundation financing caused an uproar among opposition parties and civil society groups. NGOs alluded to connections between the reluctance of the prosecutor's office to investigate the MNB funds and the fact that the wife of the prosecutor general was also a supervisory board member at two MNB foundations. On April 27, TI-H filed a criminal complaint against the MNB for misappropriation of public funds and abuse of public office; the Prosecutor General's Office declined to investigate allegations of wrongdoings committed by senior MNB officials, and despite legal requirements, failed to give a written explanation of its decision. On June 17, the MNB's supervisory board, appointed by parliament's Fidesz majority, closed an investigation into the spending of the MNB foundations, which determined there was no misconduct. On August 9, the Public Procurement Arbitration Board, a special state organization empowered to rule in public procurement cases and levy fines in case of breaches of law, found that 66 out of 112 contracts of the foundations violated the law because no bids were invited, and fined the foundations 84 million forints ($300,000). As of November, no criminal investigations had been initiated in the case.

On March 3, the Corruption Research Center Budapest released a report, *Competitive Intensity and Corruption Risks*, which concluded that in 2009-2015 public procurement was characterized by a reduction in competition, an increase in the number of procurements without competition, reduced transparency, and an increasing tendency toward price distortion and corruption risks. The report also found that EU-funded procurements had worse performance, in terms of corruption risks, competitive intensity, and transparency, than Hungarian-funded ones. The report concluded that the EU funds fostered the practice of political favoritism and fueled crony capitalism. During the year TI-H also asserted that the phenomenon of overpricing was one of the most widespread forms of corruption affecting the use of EU funds. According to TI-H, this phenomenon could affect more than 90 percent of the projects financed from EU funds and amount in an average of 20-25 percent compared to market prices.

<u>Financial Disclosure</u>: The law requires members of parliament, the most senior government officials, the president of the Curia and his deputies, and the prosecutor general to publish asset declarations on a regular basis. Asset declarations by cabinet members' spouses are not made public. The vast majority of public-sector employees, including law enforcement and army officers, judges, prosecutors, civil servants, and public servants, are obliged to submit asset declarations, but their declarations are not publicly accessible. There are no criminal or administrative sanctions for submitting inaccurate asset declarations. NGOs continued to contend the regulation was not adequate because there was no effective method to detect and sanction violators.

<u>Public Access to Information</u>: The constitution and law provide both citizens and foreigners the right to access information held by public bodies. The law provides that the bodies controlling such information may restrict access to protect what they determine to be legitimate public interests, as defined by law. The legal list of exceptions includes information on national security, prevention and prosecution of crimes, protecting nature and the environment, national financial matters, foreign affairs, active legal procedures, and intellectual property. In addition, citizens may not submit requests for an "overarching, invoice-based," or "itemized" audit of the "management of a public authority." The law also permits the state organ controlling the information to determine and charge "labor input costs associated with completing the information request," if providing the information would require "a disproportionate use of the labor resources." The amount of these charges is not communicated in advance to the requesting party. Data in a copyrighted work may be examined (and notes made thereof), but the work may not be copied, and access may be denied if the government finds that the disclosure of the requested data would endanger future government decision making.

On June 8, parliament amended the law governing financial disclosures of state-owned enterprises and economic associations that use public funds. According to the amendment, such companies may restrict access to data related to their business operations if the accessibility of such data would result in disproportionate harm. The law states that disproportionate harm results if the business rivals of the state-owned enterprise or the company using public assets would benefit from an undue and undeserved advantage through the accessibility of the data concerned. TI-H overtly criticized the law for decreasing transparency of the use of public assets.

Freedom of information requests may be submitted in oral or written form. Public bodies are required to disclose information within 15 days of receiving a request. In cases in which a significant amount of data is requested, the public body is entitled to extend the deadline for disclosure by an additional 15 days. Requesters may appeal denials in court within 30 days or initiate the procedure of the National Authority for Data Protection and Freedom of Information (NAIH). The law punishes the illicit use of public information with imprisonment for up to three years.

Domestic and international NGOs continued to criticize the regulations on access to public information, noting that they give state institutions with data management responsibilities excessive latitude to reject requests for public information and to levy arbitrary charges on requesters.

As of October, the NAIH received 409 freedom of information petitions, 156 of which resulted in investigations that identified an infringement. Of the 409 petitions, 136 sought guidance on interpretation of the law.

Section 5. Governmental Attitude Regarding International and Nongovernmental Investigation of Alleged Violations of Human Rights

A number of domestic and international human rights groups generally operated without government restrictions, investigating and publishing their findings on human rights cases. Senior government officials, however, continued the political smear campaign against human rights NGOs that began in 2013 and continued after the 2014 national elections. Meanwhile, some other government officials and Fidesz executives specifically invited some of the same human rights NGOs to consult on certain key legislative proposals.

On February 16, the UN special rapporteur on the situation of human rights defenders, Michel Forst, released a statement upon the completion of his visit to the country. In the statement, Forst concluded that "because of the disrupted checks and balances and feeble political opposition, human rights defenders who criticize the government or raise human rights concerns are quickly intimidated and portrayed as 'political' or 'foreign agents.' They face enormous pressure through public criticism, stigmatization in the media, unwarranted inspections, and reduction of state funding." Forst's final report on the visit remained pending.

On May 20 in a radio interview, Prime Minister Viktor Orban stated that organizations sponsored by Hungarian-American business executive George Soros were a "background power" that "constantly aims to gain political influence and effectively influences political decision making, according to the natural rules of democracy." On May 25, the minister of the Prime Minister's Office, Janos Lazar, stated to the press that "the entire domestic promigrant civil sector belongs to the sphere of influence of Soros" and referred to purported reports by the intelligence services substantiating his claim. On September 26, Szilard Nemeth, a Fidesz parliamentarian and deputy chairman of parliament's national security committee, stated in an interview that he had asked the committee and the country's clandestine services to examine the activities and operations of those domestic NGOs that cooperated with the Soros-funded network. Nemeth also stated he had identified 22 such organizations to be examined. On October 3, the national security committee discussed the proposal during a closed meeting. On November 17, during his weekly press conference, Lazar stated that he "considered the activity of the Soros empire in Hungary dangerous and would find it beneficial if the national security services paid specific attention to that."

On June 29, the Budapest Metropolitan Court of Appeals issued a legally binding ruling that stated the governing Fidesz party tarnished the good reputation of the HHC and ordered the party to publicly apologize and pay one million forints ($3,580) compensation for the NGO. The ruling prohibited the party from committing further rights violations. The case stemmed from a May 2015 Fidesz press statement claiming that the "bogus civil group Helsinki Committee executes the political orders of the international speculative financial capital and shamelessly attempts to falsify plain figures." The June 29 ruling also noted that the Fidesz party had repeatedly violated the HHC's right to reputation, since the court had already issued a similar ruling in June 2015 in a case where the Fidesz spokesperson called the HHC and other organizations "fake NGOs."

On October 13, officials from the National Tax and Customs Authority, without warning, searched the offices of Energia Klub, an environmental group, and seized hundreds of documents and computer files related to a climate adaptation training program that the group had implemented earlier in the year. The program was funded by the Norwegian/ European Economic Area Grants NGO fund under a climate change adaptation program and administered by the Regional Environment Center. Energia Klub filed a complaint with the Pest County Prosecutor's Office against the house search, which was rejected on November 11. According to the prosecutor's office, Energia Klub was not a suspect in the investigation and the house search was conducted in a lawful manner. On November 25, the Energia Klub appealed the prosecutor's office rejection at the court, which remained pending.

On April 27, the chair of parliament's legislative committee and Fidesz vice-president Gergely Gulyas invited leaders of three leading human rights NGOs (TI-H, the HCLU, and the HHC) to a meeting to discuss draft counterterrorism legislation and took notes of their professional recommendations. The NGOs regarded the meeting as the potential opening of a long-closed channel of communication. During the year the Ministry of Justice invited human rights NGOs to contribute to the draft of the new criminal procedure code.

Government Human Rights Bodies: The constitution and law establish a unified system for the Office of the Commissioner for Fundamental Rights (ombudsman). The ombudsman has two deputies, one responsible for the rights of national minorities and one for the interests of the "future generations" (environmental protection). The ombudsman is elected by a two-thirds majority of parliament after being proposed by the president. The ombudsman is solely accountable to parliament and has authority to initiate proceedings to defend the rights of citizens from violations committed by government institutions, banks, businesses, and social organizations. The constitution provides that citizens may submit constitutional complaints about laws passed by parliament to the ombudsman, who may request a review by the Constitutional Court. Since 2014 the ombudsman was responsible for collecting electronically submitted reports of public benefit, e.g., whistleblower reports on public corruption. The ombudsman must forward these reports to the appropriate public offices within eight days. Starting in January 2015, the ombudsman operated the national preventive mechanism prescribed by the OPCAT. By the end of September, the ombudsman had received 258 reports of public interest from citizens, 64 requests to review the activities of organs investigating reports of public interest, and 60 petitions requesting he refer laws to the Constitutional Court and had released seven OPCAT reports. As of October, the ombudsman had not filed any petitions with the Constitutional Court.

The 12-member Judiciary Committee was responsible for covering the human rights and religious portfolio in parliament. The Parliamentary Committee of the Nationalities of Hungary consisted of the spokespersons of the 13 officially recognized ethnic nationalities and was responsible for assessing legislation concerning minorities.

Section 6. Discrimination, Societal Abuses, and Trafficking in Persons

Women

<u>Rape and Domestic Violence</u>: Rape, including spousal rape, is illegal. Under the law, the definition of rape is based on the use of force or coercion and not on the lack of consent. The definition of rape also includes the exploitation of a person who is incapable of self-defense or unable to express his/her will. Penalties for rape range from two years in prison to 15 years in aggravated cases.

The criminal code includes "violence within partnership" (domestic violence) as a separate category of offense. By law, certain cases of regularly committed physical assault, defamation, violation of personal freedom, and coercion are more severely punished if the offender and the victim live together or have lived together or if a child was born as a result of their relationship. The offense relates not only to relatives and dependents but also to former spouses, relatives who live in the same domicile, common-law partners, those under guardianship or care, guardians, and caretakers. The law penalizes humiliation, causing severe deprivation to--or grave violation of--the dignity of a relative or a dependent with up to two years' imprisonment. Certain forms of economic violence are also punishable. Regulations extend prison sentences for assault (light bodily harm) and defamation to three years if committed in the above context. Grievous bodily harm, violation of personal freedom, or coercion may be punishable by one to five years in prison. If committed in a domestic violence context, malicious assault and assault committed against those incapable of self-defense or against an elderly or person with disabilities are also punishable by one to five years' imprisonment.

Police and courts may impose restraining orders. By law, police called to a scene of domestic violence may issue an emergency restraining order valid for three days in lieu of immediately filing charges, while courts may issue up to 60-day "preventive restraining orders" in civil cases. The restraining order imposed by the criminal court lasts up to 60 days without the option to extend or until the issuance of a legally binding ruling. Women's rights NGOs continued to criticize the law and its application for failing to provide appropriate protection for victims and for not placing sufficient emphasis on the accountability of perpetrators. NGOs also noted that courts and child protection authorities generally failed to recognize and take into account domestic violence in custody and visitation cases and forced visitation remained a widespread practice in the case of children with abusive parents.

On June 21, the Kecskemet Regional Court issued a legally binding ruling in the case of Jozsef Balogh, mayor of Fulophaza and former Fidesz member of parliament, for causing severe bodily harm to his common law partner in 2013. The case sparked public protests by women's groups in 2013 when the mayor blamed the family's dog for the attack. In reaction, Fidesz dismissed Balogh from the party. Balogh resigned his seat in parliament in 2013. The court sentenced Balogh to 10 months' imprisonment, suspended for two years on probation. Balogh subsequently resigned from his position as mayor.

The Ministry of Human Capacities continued to operate a 24-hour toll-free hotline for victims of domestic violence and trafficking in persons to provide information and if necessary to coordinate the immediate placement of victims in shelters. In 2015 the hotline registered 2,067 calls in relation to domestic violence, which resulted in institutional emplacement in 256 cases.

The ministry operated shelters with 98 beds at 15 locations for survivors of domestic violence, providing immediate accommodation and complex care for abused individuals and families for up to 90 days. The government also sponsored a secret shelter house with 29 beds for severely abused women whose lives were in danger, allowing a maximum stay of six months. In 2015 a total of 996 persons received assistance in the shelters. During the year the government increased funding for shelters by 50 percent and for the secret shelter house by 100 percent.

The ministry operated six halfway houses, providing long-term housing opportunities (maximum five years) and professional reintegration assistance for families graduated from shelters and assistance to prevent secondary victimization. According to women's rights NGOs, services for survivors of violence against women were not transparent, and either operated with limited capacity or did not meet international standards of good practice.

NGOs complained that, despite some positive legislative measures in recent years, a comprehensive prevention, protection, and prosecution approach was missing from the state's response to domestic violence as well as to other forms of violence against women. NGOs criticized the improper application of existing laws and regulations, the lack of systematic training and protocols for professionals, and the limited availability of proper victim support services.

Sexual Harassment: The constitution and the law establish the right to a secure workplace and make harassment a criminal offense. Penalties for harassment range from one year in prison to three years in aggravated cases. NGOs contended that the law did not clearly define sexual harassment, leaving victims with a lack of legal awareness or incentive to file a complaint. According to NGOs, sexual harassment remained widespread.

<u>Reproductive Rights</u>: Couples and individuals have the right to decide the number, spacing, and timing of their children; manage their reproductive health; and have access to the information and means to do so, free from discrimination, coercion, or violence.

Only women and men above the age of 40 or who already had three children could opt for sterilization for nonmedical reasons. Women's rights NGOs criticized the lack of state subsidy for any contraceptive method, calling it an obstacle to family planning.

<u>Discrimination</u>: The law provides for the same legal status and rights for women as for men. The Hungarian Women Lobby, the NANE Women's Rights Association, and the Patent Association asserted that Romani women could suffer from multiple discrimination on the basis of their gender, ethnicity, and class, experiencing barriers to equal access to education, health care, housing, employment, and justice.

Children

<u>Birth Registration</u>: An individual acquires citizenship from a parent who is a citizen. Births were registered immediately.

<u>Education</u>: Although the law provides for free and compulsory education between the ages of three and 16 and prohibits school segregation, NGOs reported that segregation of Romani schoolchildren continued to increase. Schools with a majority of Romani students employed simplified teaching curricula, lacked well-trained minority language teachers, were generally less well equipped, and were in significantly worse physical condition, than those with non-Romani majorities. NGOs suggested that the segregated environment and the substandard educational quality resulted in significantly lower levels of education among the Romani population. According to the Roma Education Fund, 20 percent of Romani children left the school system with a secondary school diploma (compared with 80 percent of non-Romani children) and only 2 percent obtained university diplomas in 2015.

On March 31, the deputy commissioner for fundamental rights reported to the UN Human Rights Council that, although segregation in education is prohibited by law, "in practice the segregation of Romani students was widespread." The deputy commissioner stated that the segregation was the "result of direct or indirect discriminatory practices against Romani students, while Roma minority education and religious education may also lead to segregation or malpractice."

On May 26, the European Commission began an infringement procedure against the country. The formal letter of notice to the government requested it to ensure Romani children enjoy access to quality education on the same terms as all other children and urging it to bring the national laws on equal treatment, as well as on education and the practical implementation of its educational policies, into line with EU directives.

Child Abuse: According to experts, approximately 10 percent of children under the age of 18 were beaten or assaulted. Experts generally noted significant regional disparities, with higher rates of child abuse occurring in eastern and northern sections of the country.

Efforts to combat child abuse included a "child protection signaling system" to detect and ward off factors endangering children, law enforcement and judicial measures, restraining orders, shelters for mothers and their children, and removing children from homes deemed unsafe. As of January 1, the government introduced new measures to enhance the effectiveness of the child protection signaling system, including the appointment of social workers in each town and in each district responsible for the coordination of the signaling system. Despite the changes, the public remained generally critical of the operation of the child protection system during the year. In the case of the death of an 18-month old girl in Gyongyos, on September 28, the ombudsman released a report that established serious and repeated omissions by the pediatrician, the child welfare center, and the guardianship authority leading to a failure to prevent her fatal starvation.

On December 13, parliament amended the law with a provision stating that if a parent does not "cooperate" with the doctors, district nurses, teachers, or family supporters in the signaling system, it automatically constitutes gross endangerment, even without any other signs of real negligence or endangerment.

Early and Forced Marriage: The legal minimum age of marriage is 18. The Social and Guardianship Office may authorize marriages of persons between the ages of 16 and 18.

Sexual Exploitation of Children: Buying sexual services from a child younger than 18 is a crime punishable by up to three years in prison. Forcing a child into prostitution is a crime punishable by up to three years in prison. The law prohibits child pornography. The making or distribution of pornographic images of a child is punishable by up to eight years in prison. Obtaining or having possession of pornographic images of a child is punishable by up to three years. Producing, offering, supplying, or making available pornographic images of a child is punishable by one to five years imprisonment. The sale of children is prohibited by law. The statute of limitations does not apply to sexual crimes against children. The government generally enforced the law.

The minimum age for consensual sex is 12, provided the older partner is 18 or younger. Persons older than 18 who engage in sexual relations with a minor between the ages of 12 and 14 may be punished by one to five years' imprisonment. Consensual sex between a person older than 18 and a minor between the ages of 14 and 18 is not punishable. By law, statutory rape is a felony punishable by two to eight years' imprisonment if the victim is under the age of 14 or five to 10 years' imprisonment if the victim is under the age of 12.

On November 18, the ombudsman called public attention to the extremely high discrepancy between the estimated 300,000 children exposed to some form of sexual abuse and the approximately 1,000 cases in which official procedures are initiated annually.

NGOs reported that prostitution of girls under the age of 18 remained a problem. NGOs strongly criticized the frequent practice of charging juveniles (children between the age of 14 and 18) for petty offenses and blaming the children for "prostituting themselves." Through the end of September, police initiated proceedings against 105 juveniles in connection with prostitution (10 percent of all prostitution related proceedings) as well as seven minors younger than 14. Authorities sanctioned 48 juveniles for prostitution petty offenses, including seven juveniles sentenced to imprisonment, eight to public work, 13 given fines, and 18 given warnings.

<u>Institutionalized Children</u>: According to 2011 research conducted by the European Roma Rights Center (ERRC), 66 percent of children living in state-run children's homes were of Romani origin.

NGOs continued to criticize the increasing practice by authorities of removing children from their families on the grounds of poverty or the lack of sufficient family income. The HCLU and the grassroots NGO The City Is for All claimed that such removals violated the law, which declares that children must not be removed from their families solely on the basis of economic circumstances.

The ombudsman expressed concerns that relevant professional experience was not required for persons working in childcare institutions offering special welfare services and that there was no mandatory training for such employees. During the year the ombudsman released reports on two different branches of the Karolyi Istvan Special Children's Home in Fot. A report released on February 2 on the Home for Children with Special Needs, which treats children with cognitive disabilities, established there had been violations of the prohibition of inhuman treatment in connection with the institute's failure to prevent bullying. The failure resulted from the improper set up of children's groups and the discriminatory attitudes of some caretakers. A second report release on June 13 also identified cases of inhuman treatment based on a lack of individualized assistance, the occasional practice by caretakers of separating some children from their peers, and excessive restrictions on contacts between siblings.

NGOs also criticized the lack of special assistance for child victims of human trafficking. Child victims of trafficking were placed in ordinary childcare institutions, which generally lacked trained staff and specific protocols for handling traumatized and abused children. Children could leave childcare institutions freely, which resulted in their frequent disappearance and revictimization. On March 2, the ombudsman released a report on the Zita Special Children's Home of the Somogy County Child Protection Directorate, which identified cases of inhuman treatment based on the failure of caretakers to report victims of child prostitution at the institute.

International Child Abductions: The country is a party to the 1980 Hague Convention on the Civil Aspects of International Child Abduction. See the Department of State's *Annual Report on International Parental Child Abduction* at travel.state.gov/content/childabduction/en/legal/compliance.html.

Anti-Semitism

According to estimates from the World Jewish Congress, the Jewish population numbered between 35,000 and 120,000 persons.

The Federation of Jewish Communities in Hungary (MAZSIHISZ) registered 19 incidents of anti-Semitism during the first six months of the year, one of which involved physical assault, seven involved threats, six involved hate speech, and two involved vandalism. The registered physical assault was the killing of an Israeli tourist on April 22 in Tiszakecske. Police arrested a 21-year-old man from

Kocser and a 19-year-old man from Lakitelek as suspects, and the case was pending at year's end. According to MAZSIHISZ, there were 46 anti-Semitic incidents during 2015.

The Brussels Institute, founded by TEV, continued to monitor anti-Semitism and registered 35 acts of anti-Semitism through the end of October, but no cases of physical abuse, compared to 52 anti-Semitic incidents in 2015.

On April 19, TEV published its 2015 annual report on domestic anti-Semitism, based on a survey conducted by the Median Opinion and Market Research Institute. The report concluded that approximately one-third of Hungarians harbored anti-Semitic views. The study accounted for both cognitive anti-Semitism (receptivity to stereotypes, misconceptions, and conspiracy theories) and affective anti-Semitism (emotional rejection of the Jews). The percent of extreme anti-Semites grew from 21 percent in 2014 to 23 percent in 2015, while the percentage of persons with moderately anti-Semitic views increased from 10 percent in 2014 to 12 percent in 2015.

Law enforcement and judicial agencies continued to prosecute anti-Semitic incidents. During the first nine months of the year, police registered 542 cases of vandalism in cemeteries and religious buildings (including Jewish property). On June 29, two windows of the synagogue at Gyongyos were broken with rocks thrown from the street during daytime. No injuries were reported, but property damage amounted to 500,000 forints ($1,790). Police opened an investigation for vandalism the same day, which remained pending.

On February 24, the Community of the Politically Convicted (CPC) organized the unveiling of a statue of wartime member of parliament Gyorgy Donath (1939-1944), an enthusiastic supporter of anti-Jewish legislation who was executed by the communist government in 1947 after a show trial on trumped-up charges. Several Jewish organizations and other NGOs protested the statue, which was located only a few blocks from the Holocaust Memorial Museum and Documentation Center. The district mayor's office posted an invitation to the unveiling ceremony on its official website, and governing party officials were scheduled to speak at the event. Protesters prevented the unveiling ceremony, and the CPC removed the statue two days later in response to the public outcry.

On August 18, the minister of the Prime Minister's office, Janos Lazar, issued the Knight's Cross of the Order of Merit, the state's second-highest award, to Zsolt Bayer, a controversial *Magyar Hirlap* columnist, *EchoTV* anchor, and founding

member of Fidesz, partly in recognition of his "exemplary work as a journalist."
On April 4, the Israeli ambassador to the country sent a letter of complaint to the
chief editor of *Magyar Hirlap*, claiming that a series of Bayer's articles "openly
advocate anti-Semitic sentiments and incite against the Jewish People and the State
of Israel." The ambassador asserted that Bayer's articles "not only relativize the
Shoa (Holocaust), but also make general and false accusations against the
Hungarian Jews, as if they are to be blamed for the Hungarian tragedies, which
took place through the 20th century." On May 17, the Media Council fined
Magyar Hirlap and its website in connection with a Bayer article from November
2015 that was found to promote hatred and exclusion.

Intense domestic and international criticism followed the government's decision to
decorate Bayer. More than 100 former state award recipients returned their
decorations in protest, many citing Bayer's numerous openly anti-Semitic, anti-
Roma, and otherwise racist publications. On August 25, Minister Lazar rejected
the idea of withdrawing Bayer's award and reiterated that certain aspects of his
work covering the fate of persons who were imprisoned and perished in Soviet
gulags merited state recognition (see also section 2.a., Freedom of Speech).

Numerous extreme ethnic nationalist websites continued to publish anti-Semitic
articles (see section 2.a., Internet Freedom).

According to NGOs, members of the extreme ethnic nationalist Jobbik Party
continued to limit their previous practice of making public anti-Semitic statements.
On March 30, the Debrecen Court of Appeals upheld the conviction of Tibor
Agoston, Jobbik representative on the Debrecen city council, for violating the law
prohibiting public denial of the crimes committed by national socialist or
communist regimes. The court imposed a fine of 750,000 forints ($2,690) on
Agoston for referring to the Holocaust as a "Holoscam" at a gathering in 2014.
Agoston issued a public apology in August 2015.

On September 9, the Living Memorial, a grassroots monument to commemorate
the 600,000 victims of the Holocaust in the country, was vandalized in Budapest's
Liberty Square. The perpetrators tore photographs and destroyed or stole items of
remembrance left at the memorial. The destroyed or stolen items had only
symbolic but not material value, according to the Living Memorial group, which
filed a police report on the same day; police later closed the investigation, citing
the lack of evidence of a crime.

The governmental project to establish a new Holocaust museum, the House of Fates, remained pending during the year. The project manager, widely criticized for failing to consult with Jewish communities and Holocaust experts on the content of the exhibit, officially remained in position. Senior government officials repeatedly issued assurances that the museum would be opened only if Jewish community representatives reached consensus agreement on the content of museum exhibits.

The president, the prime minister, cabinet members, and opposition politicians spoke of the culpability of the state and its officials for the Holocaust and attended events commemorating the Holocaust. On January 7, Prime Minister Viktor Orban visited the Shoes on the Danube Promenade Holocaust memorial monument and placed a candle.

Trafficking in Persons

See the Department of State's *Trafficking in Persons Report* at www.state.gov/j/tip/rls/tiprpt/.

Persons with Disabilities

The constitution and the law prohibit discrimination against persons with physical, sensory, or intellectual disabilities in employment, education, air travel and other transportation, access to health care, or the provision of other state services. NGOs continued to report that the government failed to enforce antidiscrimination laws effectively.

In harmony with the law, both the central government and municipalities continued to renovate public buildings to make them accessible to persons with disabilities. There were no data available on the percentage of government buildings that complied with the law, but NGOs asserted that many public buildings remained inaccessible.

NGOs claimed that authorities had not honored their obligation to provide public schooling to children with significant and multiple disabilities because public elementary schools are not obligated to enroll children with disabilities. The National Federation of Disabled Persons' Associations criticized the lack of accessible dormitory space for persons with disabilities at higher educational institutions.

The government continued to implement its 30-year (2011-2041) strategy to reduce the number of persons with disabilities living in institutions with capacities greater than 200 persons. In 2015 approximately 600 of 23,000 such persons moved to group homes or smaller institutions with up to 30 beds.

As of September 10, the ombudsman had released five reports on homes for elderly and mentally and physically disabled persons. On May 20, the ombudsman released a report on the Aranykor Elderly Home in Fegyvernek summarizing government site inspections at the institution, which was maintained by a nonprofit company. The report identified several instances of inhuman and degrading treatment of residents, including placing physically disabled residents on the second floor without access to an elevator; failure to employ a staff psychologist; a lack of mandatory standard procedures; holding cognitively disabled residents in permanently locked rooms; and maintaining insufficient records on the use of physical restraints. Although the institution's management corrected some key deficiencies since the inspections, the ombudsman identified further shortcomings and requested government bodies to continue monitoring the institution's operation. The other reports also identified instances of inhuman and degrading treatment at other institutions, including improper physical and hygienic conditions; lack of accessibility; overcrowding; the practice of female caretakers bathing male inhabitants; mishandling of residents' sensitive personal data; lack of privacy; staff prejudice; lack of individualized and meaningful activities for residents ; and lack of a complaint mechanism.

The constitution provides that a court may deprive persons with disabilities who are under guardianship of the right to vote due to limited mental capacity. The international NGO Mental Disability Advocacy Center continued to criticize the "mental ability" provision as an "unsophisticated disguise for disability-based discrimination" because it could apply to persons with intellectual disabilities and to persons with psychosocial disabilities. In a report released in 2014, the commissioner for human rights of the Council of Europe noted the high number of persons with disabilities who were placed under guardianship. According to the National Office for the Judiciary, 57,861 persons were under guardianship as of October 17, compared with 64,328 persons under guardianship at the end of 2015.

NGOs noted that polling places were generally not accessible to persons with disabilities. If a person was originally registered at an inaccessible polling place, he or she needed to request to be reregistered at an accessible polling station. The law also provides persons with physical disabilities the option of requesting a mobile ballot box. Persons with visual impairments have the option of requesting voting templates in Braille.

The lead agency for protecting the rights of persons with disabilities is the Ministry of Human Capacities.

National/Racial/Ethnic Minorities

Roma remained the largest ethnic minority. According to the 2011 census, approximately 315,000 persons (3 percent of the population) identified themselves as Roma. Unofficial estimates varied widely and suggested the actual figure was between 500,000 and 800,000 persons. Human rights NGOs continued to report that Roma suffered social exclusion and discrimination in almost all fields of life, particularly in employment, education, housing, prisons, and access to public places, such as restaurants and bars.

On January 12, the Curia convicted three individuals charged with the racially motivated murders of six Roma in 2008 and 2009. The Curia upheld a lower court's sentence of life imprisonment with no possibility of parole in the case of premeditated murder and other charges. In May 2015 the Budapest Metropolitan Court of Appeals sentenced the fourth defendant, who had cooperated with police during the investigation, to 13 years' imprisonment as an accomplice to the murders.

NGOs reported continued failures and omissions on the part of the police and prosecution in investigating hate crimes committed against minority group members (including Roma). On April 12, the ECHR established that the government failed to adequately investigate allegations of racially motivated abuse in the case of the Romani applicant who suffered verbal insults and threats from participants in the 2011 demonstrations organized by far-right groups in Gyongyospata. The ERRC, as third-party intervenor, asserted before the court that vulnerable victims alleging racially motivated violence were unlikely to be able to prove beyond reasonable doubt that they had been subjected to discrimination, especially when they were also victims of a failure on the part of the domestic authorities to carry out an effective investigation. The government appealed the ECHR ruling, but the Grand Chamber of the ECHR rejected the appeal on September 12 and the judgment became final.

According to the HCLU and other NGOs, in some localities (especially in Borsod-Abauj-Zemplen County) police continued to impose fines or other sanctions on

Romani residents for minor offenses that were usually ignored when committed by non-Roma, such as minor traffic infractions involving bicycles or illegal collection of firewood. The HCLU continued to report that police responses to offenses, especially in cases of petty offenses committed in the poorest regions of the country, were ethnically disproportional and often based on discriminatory ethnic profiling.

On October 24, the Hungarian Central Statistical Office released a report that stated only 39 percent of the working-age Romani population was employed in 2015 (compared to 69 percent of the non-Romani population). The government increased public employment and educational opportunities for registered unemployed persons. As of September, 327,445 persons--20 percent of whom were of Romani origin--had participated in the public employment program for at least one day. Projects typically involved cleaning public spaces or work on agricultural or water projects. Persons employed on such projects could work 12 months, which could be extended by another six months maximum. From 2012 to September 2016, approximately 195,190 public workers (including 45,559 Roma) were enrolled in an education component of the program aimed at enhancing their employability. Government statistics showed that 12.2 percent of those enrolled found employment in the primary labor market within six months of graduation from the public works program. As of September, 8,699 persons had been excluded from public employment programs for three months on the grounds that their children did not regularly attend school, they did not keep their immediate environment in order, they did not accept offered or seasonal work, or their previous labor contract was terminated with immediate effect by either the employer or the employee.

On October 24, the Hungarian Central Statistical Office released a report that stated 80 percent of the Romani population between the ages of 15 and 64 had only finished elementary school (compared to 20 percent of the non-Romani population). On May 27, a UN antidiscrimination working group stated that Romani children were largely segregated in inferior schools and continued to be placed disproportionately in schools for pupils with learning disabilities. During the 2015-16 school year, the government continued to operate Sure Start children centers providing early intervention programs for disadvantaged, mostly Romani children below kindergarten age and parenting advice for their parents. During the year, 112 such centers reached 2,507 children and their parents. From 2015 the government provided scholarships using EU funds for socially disadvantaged students, including 9,000 elementary and secondary school children and 2,285 vocational school students who declared themselves to be Roma. It also provided scholarships for socially disadvantaged higher education students, including 128 Roma. There were 171 Tanoda afterschool centers around the country providing tutoring and extracurricular activities for disadvantaged, mostly Romani children. The Tanoda network assisted approximately 3,500 disadvantaged students. There were 11 Romani special colleges across the country sponsored by the government using EU funds, seven of which were operated by Christian denominations and four managed by universities. The special colleges provided housing and tutoring for approximately 296 Romani students enrolled in higher educational institutions. The public education system continued to provide inadequate instruction for members of minorities in their own languages, and Romani language schoolbooks and qualified teachers were in short supply (see section 6, Children).

Inadequate housing continued to be a problem for Roma, whose overall living conditions remained significantly worse than those of the general population. According to Romani interest groups, municipalities continued to use a variety of techniques to prevent Roma from living in more desirable urban neighborhoods. These groups have called for the expansion of public housing.

In 2014 the local council of Miskolc adopted an urban planning decree aimed at effectively evicting approximately 3,000 residents of the city's "low comfort" neighborhoods by 2018. In April 2015 the Curia annulled the local decree on the grounds that it discriminated against persons with social needs. In July 2015 the ETA also established that the Miskolc municipality discriminated against the residents of a segregated area because of their social status, financial situation, and Romani origin. The municipality requested judicial review of the ETA decision. On January 25, the Budapest Metropolitan Public Administration and Labor Court upheld the ETA ruling and ordered the municipality to prepare an action plan to provide housing for the affected residents. On May 2, the ETA received the action plan from the Miskolc municipality outlining the April 21 city council decree on creating a social housing agency in cooperation with the Hungarian Charity Service of the Order of Malta, which would decide on placing homeless families in municipally owned properties. On June 1, a group of NGOs, joined by the Miskolc Roma self-government, issued a statement criticizing the plan for its small scale (allocating only 30 apartments while 100 families were in need) and the lack of compensation for the affected families, who had already moved from their neighborhoods due to the municipality's actions.

According to a June 2015 ombudsman report, authorities and other local bodies (i.e., public utility providers) in Miskolc jointly carried out frequent raid-like official inspection and control activities without explicit legal authorization. The raids often involved large numbers of local government police, government inspectors, and other officials descending on homes in segregated living areas populated mostly by Roma. The report asserted that the practice was incompatible with the rule of law and that individuals subjected to the inspections were unable to interpret properly the legal basis of the numerous activities that authorities conducted simultaneously, infringing on the right to fair procedures and the right to legal remedy. The ombudsman concluded that the raids resulted in direct discrimination based on social origin and financial status, and indirect discrimination based on belonging to a minority. In July 2015 the mayor of Miskolc rejected the ombudsman's report and asserted that the official control activities would continue, as the local population supported them and they were deemed necessary to control crime. In July and November 2015, the ombudsman again called on the mayor to stop the control activities. In September 2015, upon the inquiry of the ombudsman, the minister of the Prime Minister's Office stated that coordinated control activities like the one conducted in Miskolc were in accordance with the law. As of September, official control activities continued in Miskolc.

On March 21, the HCLU and the Office for National and Ethnic Minority Rights Protection filed a lawsuit against the Miskolc municipality, its Law Enforcement Department, and the Mayor's Office for the violation of personality rights in connection with discriminatory anti-Roma actions and rhetoric. The case remained pending before the Court of Miskolc.

On September 1, ODIHR released a report, *The Housing Rights of Roma in Miskolc, Hungary*, based on a June 2015 visit to Budapest and Miskolc led by ODIHR director Michael Link. In the report, ODHIR expressed "grave concerns about the allegations of discrimination in the provision of adequate housing for Roma residents of Miskolc,…the joint control activities conducted in predominantly Roma settlements with social housing, and the effects it has on the community."

To apply for EU and government funds for urban rehabilitation and public education projects, municipal authorities must attach a local equal opportunity plan outlining planned actions to eradicate segregation in housing and education. According to the Ministry of Human Capacities, during the year some 280,000 Roma lived in approximately 1,384 settlements where at least half the population were Roma. Segregated settlements lacked basic infrastructure and were often located on the outskirts of cities. During the year, the government continued a 45 billion forints ($161 million) settlement rehabilitation program to improve the living conditions of residents of segregated settlements. The program involved 198 settlements with more than 40,000 residents. The government continued implementing the National Social Inclusion Strategy 2011-20 and its 2015-2017 action plan.

The law establishes cultural autonomy for nationalities (replacing the term "minorities") and recognizes the right to foster and enrich historic traditions, language, culture, and educational rights as well as to establish and operate institutions and maintain international contacts. The law stipulates that any municipality with 30 residents belonging to a registered ethnic group may form a "nationality self-government" to organize activities and manage cultural, educational, and linguistic affairs. The president of each nationality self-government body has the right to attend and speak at local council sessions. The law provides for the 13 national minorities, including Roma, to vote for a national minority list in parliamentary elections; the Romani minority had a spokesperson in parliament (see section 3).

Acts of Violence, Discrimination, and Other Abuses Based on Sexual Orientation and Gender Identity

The law explicitly prohibits discrimination based on sexual orientation. In addition, the law prohibits certain forms of hate speech and prescribes increased punishment for violence against members of the lesbian, gay, bisexual, transgender, and intersex (LGBTI) community, specifically referencing these groups as being targeted for their "gender identity" or "sexual orientation."

On May 27, a UN antidiscrimination working group released a statement following an official visit to the country in which it expressed concern over the "incitement to hatred against sexual and gender minorities by politicians and leading government officials."

On July 2, an estimated 15,000 persons joined the annual Budapest Gay Pride Parade. Police secured the parade and sealed off the route of the march. In contrast to previous years, there was no counterdemonstration organized in protest against the parade. On November 7, the Pest Central District Court sentenced one person to three years and another to two years in prison for assaulting five persons who had taken part in the 2013 Budapest Gay Pride Parade. Three other persons received suspended prison terms.

On November 23, on the proposal of Mayor Laszlo Toroczkai (vice-president of the extreme nationalist Jobbik party), the local council of Asotthalom adopted a decree banning the promulgation of same-sex marriage and the definition of the family as anything other than marriage or parent-child relationship. The decree encompassed any activity in public space, such as demonstrations, performances, posters, flyers, and loudspeaker advertisements. On December 10, approximately 30 LGBTI activists staged a small demonstration in front of the mayor's office in the village. The demonstration was not interrupted. On December 12, the HCLU urged the ombudsman to initiate annulment of the decree at the Constitutional Court. On December 14, the Csongrad County Government Office declared the Asotthalom council decree unlawful. On December 16, the ombudsman filed a petition with the Constitutional Court seeking annulment of the decree.

Section 7. Worker Rights

a. Freedom of Association and the Right to Collective Bargaining

The law, including related regulations and statutory instruments, provides for the right of workers to form and join independent unions without previous authorization or excessive requirements, conduct their activities without interference, and bargain collectively. With the exception of law enforcement and military personnel, prison guards, border guards, health-care workers, and firefighters, workers have the right to strike. The law permits military and police unions to seek resolution of grievances in court. The law prohibits antiunion discrimination and provides for reinstatement of workers fired for union activity. The government established professional associations in the public sector where the membership of workers was compulsory.

While employers were not allowed to hire temporary workers during a strike, temporary workers hired beforehand were allowed to continue working. Workers at certain public offices or companies performing activities that authorities determine are essential to the public interest, such as schools, municipalities, public transport, telecommunications, water, power, gas, and other energy-sector firms, may not strike unless an agreement has been reached on provision of "sufficient services" during a strike. Fundamental services may not be considerably restricted, and courts determine the definition of sufficient services. National trade unions opposed the law on the basis that the courts lacked the expertise to rule on minimum service levels that are necessary and that the term "abusing the right to strike" was too vague. Unions reported courts generally refused to rule on such cases, essentially inhibiting the right to strike.

The government effectively enforced laws providing for freedom of association and collective bargaining. Penalties took the form of fines imposed by courts but were generally inadequate to deter violations. To engage in collective bargaining, the law requires trade unions to represent either 10 percent of workers employed by an employer or 10 percent of the workers covered by a collective agreement. Labor unions of law enforcement professionals are not entitled to collective bargaining rights. The law does not allow the labor inspectorate to enforce collective rights. The labor inspectorate does not use inspections, remediation efforts, or monetary penalties in enforcement efforts. Administrative and judicial procedures were sometimes subject to lengthy delays and appeals.

Authorities and employers generally respected freedom of association and the right to collective bargaining. The International Trade Union Confederation noted, however, that the labor code prohibits any worker conduct that may jeopardize the employer's reputation or legitimate economic and organizational interests and explicitly provides for the possibility of restricting the workers' personal rights in this regard--including their right to express an opinion during or outside of working hours. There was also anecdotal evidence of unilateral termination of collective agreements. Unions reported that the government continued to attempt to influence their independent operation.

The International Trade Union Confederation remained concerned that judges often delayed the registration of trade unions and that court procedures were generally long and cumbersome. While the law provides for reinstatement of workers fired for union activity, court proceedings on unfair dismissal cases sometimes took more than a year to complete, and authorities did not always enforce court decisions. Trade unions reported cases of employers intimidating trade union members; transferring, relocating, or dismissing trade union officers; and hindering union officials from entering the workplace.

b. Prohibition of Forced or Compulsory Labor

While the law prohibits all forms of forced or compulsory labor, the government failed to enforce it effectively. Government inspections and efforts to identify victims remained inadequate, despite significant efforts to eliminate trafficking. Penalties for forced labor range from one to 20 years in prison or life imprisonment in certain circumstances and were sufficiently stringent compared with other serious crimes.

Forced labor occurred throughout the year. Groups vulnerable to forced labor included those in extreme poverty, Roma, and homeless men. Women and girls were vulnerable to sex trafficking. Men typically were subjected to forced labor, especially in agriculture, construction, and factories. The government increased law enforcement efforts and sustained its prevention efforts.

Also see the Department of State's *Trafficking in Persons Report* at www.state.gov/j/tip/rls/tiprpt/.

c. Prohibition of Child Labor and Minimum Age for Employment

The constitution generally prohibits child labor. The law prohibits children younger than 16 from working, except that children who are 15 or 16 may work under certain circumstances as temporary workers during school vacations. Any person who is at least 15 years old and enrolled in full-time studies may enter into employment during school holidays. With authorization of a guardian, persons under the age of 16 may be employed to perform in cultural, artistic, sports, or advertising activities. Children may not work night shifts or overtime or perform hard physical labor. Any person who violates the provisions of the law pertaining to the employment of individuals under the age of 18 without authorization to undertake gainful employment may be punished with imprisonment not exceeding three years. No information was available about the adequacy and effectiveness of child labor law enforcement or penalties for violations.

Child labor occurred. Through the end of October, the employment authority reported three cases, involving three children, of child labor under the age of 15. The employment authority also reported two cases (involving three children) who were 15 or 16, and 14 cases (involving 21 children) between ages of 16 and 18 who were employed without the consent of their parents or legal representatives. The labor inspectorate found 10 cases, involving 11 minors, of infringement of requirements regarding underage workers' working and rest periods. Labor inspectors who identify child victims of labor exploitation are required to report them to the guardianship authority.

d. Discrimination with Respect to Employment and Occupation

The constitution and laws prohibit discrimination based on race, sex, gender, disability, language, sexual orientation and gender identity, infection with HIV or other communicable diseases, or social status. The labor code provides for the principles of equal treatment. The government failed to enforce these regulations effectively. Penalties took the form of fines but were generally inadequate to deter violations.

Discrimination in employment and occupation occurred with respect to Roma, women, and persons with disabilities. According to NGOs, there was economic discrimination against women in the workplace, particularly against job seekers older than 50 and those who were pregnant or had returned from maternity leave. Romani women were subject to discrimination on the basis of their gender, ethnicity, and class and experienced barriers to equal access to employment. A government decree requires companies with more than 25 employees to reserve 5 percent of their work positions for persons with physical or mental disabilities. While the decree provides fines for noncompliance, employers generally paid the fines rather than employ persons with disabilities. The National Tax and Customs Authority issued "rehabilitation cards" for disabled persons, which granted tax benefits for employers employing such individuals. As of July, 86,628 persons had such rehabilitation cards, of whom 26,091 were employed by 7,566 employers.

e. Acceptable Conditions of Work

The national minimum monthly wage for full-time employment was 111,000 forints ($400) per month. A special minimum monthly wage for jobs requiring the completion of secondary education was 129,000 forints ($460) per month. The 2014 poverty level was 87,300 forints ($313) per month per person.

The law sets the official workday at eight hours, although it may vary depending on industry. A 48-hour rest period is required during any seven-day period. The regular workweek is 40 hours with premium pay for overtime and two days of rest. The labor code sets the maximum limit of overtime at 250 hours per year and provides for paid annual national holidays. The government set occupational safety and health standards, which were current and appropriate for the main industries. Workers have the right to remove themselves from situations that endangered their health or safety without jeopardy to their employment, and authorities effectively protected employees in such situations. Labor laws also apply to foreign workers with work permits.

Labor standards were not enforced in all sectors, including the informal economy. Information regarding penalties and their sufficiency to deter violations was not available. The employment authority and the labor inspectorate units of government offices monitored and enforced occupational safety and health standards and labor code regulations. As of September, occupational safety inspectors registered 16,557 injuries at workplaces, most of them in the mechanical engineering and manufacturing industries. The number of workplace injuries included 60 fatalities, most of which took place in the agricultural, construction, and logistics sectors.